W. S. W. S. Reading Course '53-54 ①

Spiritual Life

In Quest of
God's Power

In Quest of God's Power

CHARLES L. ALLEN

Fleming H. Revell Company
WESTWOOD, N. J.
LOS ANGELES · LONDON · GLASGOW

FIRST EDITION

Printed in the United States of America

Westwood, N. J.—316 Third Avenue
Los Angeles 41—2173 Colorado Boulevard
London E. C. 4—29 Ludgate Hill
Glasgow C. 2—229 Bothwell Street

For

LEILA HAYNES ALLEN

my wife and best friend

for eighteen years

Appreciation is expressed to
The Atlanta *Journal-Constitution*
for permission to use the material in this book.

Contents

Where Many Have Found That Power

An average of thirty thousand people a year kneel and pray at the altar of Grace Methodist Church in Atlanta at the close of the Sunday night services. It is a thrilling experience to see this church, located in the heart of a great city, filled every Sunday night with people "in quest of God's power." And at the altar many have found His power.

When I was appointed pastor of Grace I was somewhat bewildered. I had started my ministry in country churches and in small towns. My father was a country preacher; I had never lived in a city and knew nothing about a city church.

On the Saturday afternoon before I was to preach my first sermon at Grace, I went to look at the sanctuary. No one was there but me. The building seemed so big and I so little that I felt hopelessly lost and inadequate. I walked down the aisle and knelt at the altar. I cannot explain it, but while kneeling there talking with God, a great peace came into my heart. As I left the church that afternoon, I was no longer worried nor afraid.

On Sunday night I told the congregation of my experience and offered an opportunity for others to come and pray at the altar; many did come and every Sunday night since many more have knelt there. Out of a congregation which averages about a thousand a night, some six hundred come to the altar.

In just four years the membership of the church has doubled and the yearly budget increased from $19,000 to $150,000. Plans are now being drawn to enlarge the building and the church program of activities. It is truly a church built by people "in quest of God's power" and who found that power on their knees at the altar.

This book is taken from my Sunday night sermons, which were later published in the Atlanta *Journal-Constitution*.

CHARLES L. ALLEN

Atlanta, Georgia

In Quest of
God's Power

The Person You Can Be

"PLEASE WRITE TELLING how one can become sure of himself," is characteristic of the requests for advice I have received. Learning to become sure of one's self is one of the very important lessons to be learned in the school of life. The first essential is to realize what a marvelous creature one is.

Men have developed some amazing machines but never has man been able to create a machine that can be even remotely compared with man himself. For example, think of what a wonderful air-conditioning system each of us possesses. The average person develops 2500 calories a day, which is enough heat to boil twenty-five pots of coffee.

The brain has a thermostat with its own nervous system which is in continuous contact with every part of the body. If part of the body gets too hot or too cold, signals are sent to the control center to notify the blood vessels of the skin to contract or dilate in order to give off more or less heat, as may be required. Perspiration occurs when additional cooling is required. No air-conditioning system man has developed is anywhere near as perfect as the one built in the human body.

The electrical system of the body is beyond imagination. The human brain contains ten million neurons (nerve cells). Each of these neurons in the brain is capable of operating at a potential of .07 volt.

The eyes are connected with the brain by 300,000 separate and private "telephone" lines. When you look at a vase of flowers, thousands of separate and distinct messages are sent to your brain telling you the size and shape of each one, the variations in color, etc.

Inventors have used all their skill to develop a mechanical hand, but their best efforts have produced clumsy results. All the mechanical genius in the world can never develop a hand that can play an organ, paint a picture, or perform a delicate surgical operation. Yet, normally, each of us is born with not one but two hands.

When you go to a photographer to have your picture made, he must make a number of adjustments on his camera. Your eye has all the adjustments of the most expensive camera and many more, but these adjustments are made automatically and instantaneously. Each of your eyes contains a hundred million nerve cells, which work together perfectly to allow you to see close up, at a distance, and in color.

The average piano has a keyboard with eighty-eight keys. But you have a keyboard with fifteen hundred keys in each ear. The ear is so sensitive that, in a completely sound-proof room, you can actually hear the blood flowing through your vessels.

The work horse of the body is the heart. In the body are about a hundred thousand miles of blood vessels, a vast system through which the heart keeps the blood flowing regularly. To do that, a normal heart beats about a hundred thousand times a day. But normally you need never worry about your heart being overworked, because it rests a sixteenth of every second. This totals up to a rest of about six hours a day or about twenty years during a normal lifetime.

Most wonderful of all the instruments of the body is the mind. It completely defies comparison. It gives you the ability to think and to reason, to remember and to plan.

As you think of yourself, you begin to say with the Psalmist, "I am fearfully and wonderfully made" (139:14). And that leads you to a more sublime thought. You probably have a watch. It is an intricate mechanism.

How did that watch come to be? It was made. And if it was made, then it had to have a maker. So you say with the Bible, "All things were made by him; and without him was not anything made" (John 1:3). "All things" include you. You can know that back of your life is a maker. We call Him God.

As you realize that you were planned and made, you become sure of the existence of a personal God. And as you begin to use and develop your marvelous self, you become surer of God and thereby surer of yourself.

As a result of my talks with hundreds of unhappy and defeated people, I have come to the conclusion that the four main obstacles to personal development and power are these: self-pity, false pride, a martyr complex, and a sense of inferiority.

However, Christ gave us some words that, if faithfully applied, will be a sure cure for any one or all of these ills. The cure is: "Go ye . . . lo, I am with you" (Matthew 28:19,20). Let us look at them one by one.

(1) Self-pity. One of the easiest things in the world is to feel sorry for yourself. When one is disappointed or defeated, it is indeed soothing to indulge in an overdose of self-sympathy. But it will destroy your determination and rob you of your self-respect.

But when one begins to say over and over to himself, "God told me to go and He promised to go with me," one begins to live again and to look straight at himself. He asks, Why has my life bogged down? Is it circumstances beyond my control? No. Has God failed me? No. It is simply that I have not done my best.

Instead of feeling sorry for himself, he begins to say, I am going to quit pretending. Instead of a nurse, I need a boss, and I am going to be that boss. No matter what has happened, there is something in life for me, and, with God's help, I will find it.

(2) False pride. This is one of the great enemies of the soul. It keeps you from admitting to others that your attitudes and actions have been wrong, from confessing to yourself your own weaknesses and mistakes. Pride gives you a false sense of values and it closes to you the door to the blessed life.

Pride tells you that you are self-sufficient and destroys your humility. You try to make it with only your own strength, and you pay no attention to, "Lo, I am with you." You block out God's power.

(3) A martyr complex. It is so easy to feel you are carrying burdens greater than anyone else has borne, to

parade your sorrows and difficulties and develop an almost insane desire for sympathetic attention.

Just as some people become addicted to liquor or dope, others become addicted to sympathy and praise. Because one is afraid or unwilling to face life as it really is, he invents all sorts of misfortunes to gain appreciation. This is the reason so many people "enjoy" poor health.

But when one becomes conscious of a sense of mission and, with the support of the power of God, begins to fulfill that mission, he doesn't need to be a martyr.

(4) A sense of inferiority. The basic cause of inferiority is a comparison of ourselves with others. But when one is convinced that he has a purpose in life, that God has given him the necessary abilities and is helping him to accomplish that purpose, then no matter what any other person is or does, there comes into one's heart a sense of personal satisfaction that eliminates envious comparisons.

When these four enemies are eliminated, a marvelous change takes place. A simple technique that I have suggested to a number of people is this: Whenever you face a difficulty or whenever you are confused, don't give up and start running away. Instead, start asking over and over, "What would Christ do?"

That works wonders, because it makes you feel that Christ would do something and, if He would do something, it means that something can be done. Before you know it, you will find a solution that is practical and that you can carry through. You become baptized with self-respect, and you have a sense of tremendous, undefeatable support.

One of the top Canadian athletic coaches is Ace Percival. He has devoted some thirty-eight years to a scientific analysis of sports, and he contends that nearly every boy could be an outstanding athlete if he applied himself to it in the right manner. And he further contends that his rules will apply equally as well in building an outstanding life. The rule that he puts first is "Don't be a hold out."

By that he means, give your very best to the task before you. My father gave me a valuable lesson in this respect soon after I started preaching. I was telling him how hard it was for me to prepare a sermon. I had not read much and had had very little experience, and thus had not much to say.

During the conversation, I told him of an unusually good illustration for a sermon I had read the week before. He asked why I did not use that in my sermon the next Sunday. I told him I was saving that for a special occasion. Very gently but very firmly he said, "Now, son, every time you preach is a special occasion. Put the best you have into your next sermon and then you will get something else."

I have followed that advice. Many preachers maintain an elaborate filing system for their sermon materials, but I don't. Every week I put the best I have into my sermons, saving nothing back for the next week, and I believe that system has worked well for me.

I know women who have beautiful linens but have saved them for thirty years. Others have kept lovely china carefully put away and through the years have eaten out of cracked, cheap plates. Why have nice things if they are always too nice to use? Saving is a virtue that can become a fault.

Not long ago a good friend of mine, Mr. Roy Sewell, gave me a suit of clothes. It is the nicest and most expensive suit I have ever had. In fact, it has become a problem to me. I go out of town a great deal, but I would not want to wear that suit while traveling. On the other hand, if I put it in my bag it would get wrinkled, and I don't want that to happen. It is too good to wear every day. So I am in danger of saving my good suit to death.

We do that same thing with ourselves. We hold out our best because we think the opportunity immediately before us is not big enough. I remember hearing Dr. Willis A. Sutton tell how, as a young man, he taught a Sunday-school class in a small country church. Most of the time he had just one pupil in the class. But he carefully prepared his lesson and gave it his best.

That one pupil later became a bishop in the Methodist Church and Dr. Sutton became known as one of the best teachers of our generation. Today there are thousands of former students of his who have risen up and called his name blessed. But even in a very small opportunity he was not a hold out. He gave his best to whatever task was before him, even though it was just one pupil in a country Sunday-school class.

I lead the singing in my church on Sunday nights. I really do not know how to lead, so actually I just announce the hymn, after which it is every man for himself. But I enjoy watching a large congregation sing. Some do not try at all, others make a half-hearted attempt, but there are some who sing as if their lives depended on it.

They do not hold back, and the result is, they create an enthusiastic atmosphere in the service and they enjoy it greatly themselves. But for the hold outs the service does not mean much.

A lot of people have talked to me who were unhappy in their jobs. They feel qualified for much larger responsibilities than they have. But I pointed out to them this principle of being a hold out, suggesting that they put their first-rate abilities into even a second-rate job. Some have done just that, with amazing results.

Ace Percival says that people have a tendency to hold too much of themselves in reserve; they don't invest a hundred per cent of themselves in competition. He has been a builder of great athletic teams because he could inspire the athlete to give his best.

Jesus said, "He that findeth his life shall lose it; and he that loseth his life for my sake shall find it" (Matthew 10:39). That is, when you find something big enough to completely give yourself to, you will at the same time find a great life for yourself. There are many people who are hold outs, saving themselves to death.

To me, Abraham Lincoln is the embodiment of what makes a person great. Some people have said that I look like Lincoln. We all know that he was the homeliest looking man who ever lived, but if your thoughts can influence how you look, then it is possible that I might resemble him slightly because I have read and studied his life as I have read and studied the life of no other American.

One of the greatest things he ever said was to a group of boys: "You boys must always thank the good God that you have been born in a country where, if you will lead a decent, clean life, trust God and work hard, you can rise, and the only thing that will limit you is your industry, your character, and your brain."

Of course, the story of his own life is our greatest example of that truth. Born in humble circumstances, he acquired early in life the name of "Honest Abe." He was not afraid of hard work, he trusted God, and rose to be the greatest American of all time.

We need a Lincoln today. We need the emphasis Lincoln placed on human values. When I was in high school I learned his Gettysburg address by heart, and delivered it with all the stress in the wrong places. It was only recently that I learned how Lincoln really said it.

I would say, "Government *of* the people, *by* the people . . ." That is not what Lincoln said. He said, "Government of the *people,* by the *people* . . ." It is the people that is important. That is where Lincoln's emphasis always was.

One day I rode in a fine new car. I was fascinated by it. Touch a button, and the window would come down. Touch another button, and the radio aerial would go up.

Riding along in that car, I began thinking of all the fine things we now have. Then I realized that there are a lot of people today who have come to think that cars are more important than human beings, that mechanical gadgets are greater than human values.

Lincoln would forcibly remind us that what we *are* is far more important than what we *have.*

I bow to no person in my love and loyalty to the South. My grandfather was wounded on Kennesaw Mountain and limped the remainder of his life. My great-grandfather fought the entire war for his beloved South and, on his weary way home to North Georgia, died in Atlanta and was buried in Oakland Cemetery.

But we need to remember that Lincoln saw people who he felt were being mistreated, and he could not help but proclaim their emancipation. Yet, through all the bitterness, it was "with malice toward none, with charity toward all."

February 12 is also the birthday of Immanuel Kant, the great philosopher, who was born just five years before Lincoln. And the thinking of the two men was remarkably similar in many respects.

Immanuel Kant summed up his philosophy in one sentence: "Two things fill me with ever-increasing admiration and awe, the longer and more earnestly I reflect upon them: the starry heavens without and the moral law within."

We are all thrilled by the "heavens that declare the glory of God." But, equally sublime, said the great thinker, is that something within a man that makes him a person instead of an animal.

Recently somebody sent me a book entitled, *How to Sell Yourself*. There are dozens of books of that type on the market. Books on how to develop our personality, how to succeed, etc., are best sellers today.

But Lincoln said it so much better, and he did not need to write a book to say it. "Live a decent, clean life, work hard and trust God."

I talk to a lot of people whose lives have become

mixed up and unhappy. Many of us are in bad shape because we thought there were short cuts to success.

Lincoln gave us the three fundamentals:

A clean life. Someone has well said, "Wrong is wrong even if everybody is doing it. Right is right even if nobody is doing it." There is no substitute for fundamental right living.

Hard work. A man once said to Thomas A. Edison, "You are a genius." He replied, "Before I was a genius, I was a slave." There are no easy, effortless pathways to greatness.

Trust God. The record is that night after night Lincoln fell on his face in the White House, dug in the carpet with his long, bony fingers, and agonized before God to save this nation.

He did not pray that God would be on his side; he prayed that he might be on God's side.

There is a mysterious something about the Christian faith that I suppose we will never understand. Like the X-ray, we know how to use it, and we know the results we can obtain with it, yet no person knows exactly what it is. We light up a room with electricity but no man can explain what electricity is.

While I cannot explain the marvelous power of the Christian faith, I do know it does work miracles in a human life, and I can point out the steps by which one can obtain that faith.

A blind man named Bartimæus was sitting by the side of the road begging. He was making no contribution to the world in which he was living. He took part in no worth-while movements. He had become a liability to his fellow men. He had become a parasite.

Worse still, he had become reconciled to his futile way of life and had given up to hopelessness. His morale had slowly deteriorated. The story does not specifically say so, but people are about the same in every generation, and we know that when one ceases to contribute to life, his character is soon destroyed.

Long since this man had ceased to live constructively, and the one thought in his mind every time he heard a footfall on the highway was, "What can I get out of this person?" Thus the affliction of his character became much worse than his affliction of physical blindness.

But one day Bartimæus became dissatisfied with himself. That is the first important step to take in obtaining the power of faith. So long as one is content with his condition, even Christ cannot help him. Some passerby probably dropped a penny in the beggar's clutching fingers and then, seeing the miserable state of the man, said, "Why don't you get up from there and amount to something?"

"Don't mock me," Bartimæus probably whined. "I am blind. I cannot do anything." Then the man might have told some of the miracles he had seen—the dead daughter of Jairus brought back to life, the ten lepers who were healed, the five thousand fed with a boy's lunch, other blind men whose sight had been restored. The man responsible for all these miracles was a man named Jesus.

With such power abroad in the land, Bartimæus began to believe that he, too, might be healed. One of the basic laws of science is what has been done, can be done.

So there was no longer any reason for hopelessness. If he could get to Jesus he could be healed.

Then he began to pray. He did not mumble some nice, pious little prayer. The story says, "He began to cry out." There were some around him who were shocked at his undignified behavior and "charged him that he should hold his peace." But Bartimæus is determined to be heard. In his desire to be healed, he rises above his pride.

Those are the first three steps: be dissatisfied with yourself, believe there is one who can help you, seek that help.

Now the fourth step is made by Christ. The call of the beggar is heard and returned. "Be of good comfort, rise; he calleth thee." On the authority of the truest book ever written, we can say that when we call on God's help in the right spirit, He always hears and responds. A prayer backed up by a sense of need and faith is always answered in the very wisest way. There is never an exception.

Before the wonderful healing, Bartimæus must do one thing more. Notice carefully the wording: "And he, casting away his garment, rose, and came to Jesus." That garment was a hindrance to him in coming to Christ, so he left it behind.

There are sins and sinful habits that block our spiritual progress. Before God can forgive it, we must forsake it. There is our selfishness, the fear of what others might say or think, the unwillingness to accept the discipline of discipleship. Many things which are not harmful in themselves, even good things, hinder the best. These things must be surrendered.

St. Paul went even further. Even though it did not hinder him, if he was accustomed to doing something that hindered some weaker person, he gave up the habit (I Corinthians 8:13).

The story ends: "And immediately he received his sight, and followed Jesus in the way." He sat by the side of the way no longer. Instead, he put his feet on the highway and marched with the procession (Mark 10:46-52).

Handicaps Need Not Handicap

Unless you are a very rare exception, you are handicapped in some way. There are some 16 million deaf or hard-of-hearing people in the United States. Many more than that number need eyeglasses. Millions are crippled in some form or have some bodily illness or ailment.

Then there are the vast uncounted numbers who are mentally handicapped in one form or another. Still others are handicapped by circumstances, as, for example, the large number who did not have a fair chance to get a formal education, and those who have unusual family responsibilities that prevent their doing many things they would like to do.

Unfortunately, too many people let their handicaps chain them to inertia or despair. They become unable to reach for the best in life. Others turn their handicaps into blessings.

Psychologists recognize a law they call the law of overcompensation. Realizing his handicap, the victim works much harder than he would have attempted without his affliction, and often rises to heights of achievement that the rest of us well may emulate.

One of the funniest books I have read is Clarence Day's *Life With Father.* Yet when he wrote that book, Mr. Day's fingers were so crippled with arthritis that he could not hold a pencil. He would have someone tie a pencil on his fingers so that he could write.

Julius Cæsar had epilepsy, Charles Darwin was an invalid, Lord Nelson had only one eye, Beethoven became deaf, John Milton became blind, Charles Steinmetz was a hunchback, Robert Louis Stevenson had tuberculosis, yet all of them overcame disadvantage and reached the fulfillment of their dreams. Their handicaps became spurs to achievement.

In Fort Valley, Georgia, where I spent several days holding some special revival services, I met two ladies who are wonderful examples of the law of overcompensation. One is Mrs. Bob Berry. She was in a rolling chair, badly and painfully crippled with arthritis. She had eagerly looked forward to these services and had planned to attend. But this week she was not in condition to be carried.

However, instead of letting her disappointment make her bitter, she began saying, "I cannot go, so I must find something else to do to help." So she would have someone roll her chair out on the porch and would call to all who passed on the sidewalk and urge them to attend the services. I think she helped the revival as much as anybody in town.

The other lady I came to know is Miss Angeline Kupfer. She is a most charming young lady about twenty years old. However, she is badly handicapped. She was born without forearms. On her elbows she has what may be termed half-hands, with only one finger on each. Also, she was born with only one leg.

But don't waste any sympathy on her; she doesn't need it. She finished school with honors. She learned, of all things, to type and passed the state merit test. Now she is the clerk in the Peach County Health Department. She drives her own car and one of her favorite sports is swimming. At night she sells tickets in the drive-in theater.

More impressive than her accomplishments, however, is her spirit. I could detect no trace of self-pity in her and no resentment. She is not sensitive. And on her face is a radiant smile that makes me feel good every time I see her. She is one of the happiest people I know.

Western Electric made a study of 1400 of its employes. Seven hundred were noticeably handicapped, while 700 had no apparent handicap. They were all judged on the basis of production, labor turn-over, and absenteeism. On every count the handicapped were superior.

St. Paul had a handicap which he referred to as "a thorn in the flesh." Three times he prayed that God might take it away. But God answered Paul, "My Grace is sufficient for thee: for my strength is made perfect in weakness" (II Corinthians 12:9). Because of his handicap, Paul became a stronger and a better man.

So, if you have a handicap, take heart and take hope, because handicaps need not handicap.

One day I spoke over the radio on "What to Do When You Get Sick." I soon had opportunity to test my preaching, because the very next week I myself was sent unexpectedly to a hospital.

In my radio talk I said that when a person is sick he should do three things. First, go to a physician and tell him all the facts as best he can, and then do exactly what the doctor advises.

I followed that advice. I felt a sudden pain in my back. The pain was of sufficient intensity to make me aware that something was wrong. The doctor told me to go immediately to the hospital for two weeks. Now, going to the hospital was the last thing I wanted to do. I had a number of appointments that I had to fill, but I followed my doctor's advice and recovered. I felt even better than I had felt before my illness.

It looks as if any person would go to a physician when he is sick, but many do not. A doctor in Atlanta told me only recently that cancer could almost be stamped out if people were not afraid of it. Many suspect that they have cancer but will not go to a physician for fear he will confirm their suspicion. Too often the delay is fatal.

Dr. Ernest Thomas tells of a man who was obsessed by the fear that he was losing his hearing. He refused to see a doctor for fear that he would have to wear a hearing aid. So he struggled against the pall of silence gathering about him. He even resorted to carrying on conversations in writing so that he would not have to struggle to hear. The poor man was almost out of his mind. He was about to lose his position and everything he had. Finally, he was forced to see a physician. After a careful examination, the doctor made the astounding diagnosis that the man's ears were only stopped up. He cleaned them out and in less than a week the sufferer's hearing was fully restored.

Second, if you really are sick, make the most of it. It may be the greatest blessing of your life. I really relished those two weeks in the hospital. I rested a lot, gained several pounds, caught up on a lot of back reading, and enjoyed life in general. My illness caused me to change most of my plans for the summer, but I made other plans that were much better.

When one thinks of flowers and plants, he thinks of Luther Burbank. But if Burbank had not been sick we would never have heard of him. As a young man he was a semi-invalid. Worse still, he was filled with the fear that because of his illness he would be a failure in life.

Finally, he changed his employment. He had been working in a hot, dusty factory in Worcester, Massachusetts. He quit that job and went to work in a plant nursery. But those long New England winters further weakened his sick body. He then moved to California. He worked with plants out-doors in that warm climate, regained his health, and became one of the world's greatest naturalists.

It was Burbank who said, "Every weed can be made a flower." Had it not been for his sickness, he would have spent his days in a hot, dusty factory.

Even if sickness does come your way, don't throw up your hands in panic or bitter resentment. It might be your greatest blessing.

Third, when you are sick, let God relieve the strain and tension in your mind. I refer to the story of Jesus stilling the tempest (Mark 4:35-41). It looked as though the ship would sink and the disciples said to Jesus, "Carest thou not that we perish?" They were not the last people to wonder if God cares.

Very calmly Jesus said, "Peace, be still," and the wind ceased. And when storms arise in our own lives, He can bring us peace and serenity.

Faith in Him assures us that, somehow, somewhere, things will work out all right. It does not always take away the pain, but it does give power to endure the pain. Put yourself in His hands.

At some time in our lives all of us will have some personal troubles. In talking with many who have been defeated by their troubles I have discovered that defeat is usually the result of following a certain pattern. I shall outline it here. When trouble comes, one has a tendency to feel that he has been unfairly singled out and that his misfortune is different from that of any other person's. In a sense, that is true. Your trouble is different because you are different, and though many others have experienced similar trouble, still, it is new to you.

In such a case there is a real temptation to sympathize with yourself. After all, you have sympathized with many others in sorrow or misfortune, and it is natural to turn some sympathy in one's own direction. Thinking of your sympathy for others over the years, you have a tendency to feel that now in your own woe you are not receiving the sympathetic understanding from others which you deserve.

So, before you realize it, you begin to pity yourself. Self-pity is a form of mental and spiritual dope. It becomes habit forming, and, little by little, you feel the need of more and more. You want more pity than you can supply, so you begin seeking the pity of others.

Then we begin to tell our woes to every ear that will listen. Bishop Arthur Moore tells about a boyhood friend of his who had a sore thumb. He kept a big bandage on it, and he would say to every person he met, "Do you want to see my sore thumb?" Then he would start unwinding the big bandage. Many people enjoy baring their troubles because of the pity they receive.

Little by little, we completely surrender to our troubles and soon begin to feel they will continue. In fact, we can reach the point where we want them to continue. Not being able to accomplish the things in life that others have accomplished, our afflictions become a welcome excuse for failure. Thus we can complacently content ourselves with a life far short of our dreams, ambitions, and abilities.

We can reach the point where we had rather keep our troubles than do something about them. Recently I had a slight toothache. It was not so bad that I could not stand it. I knew that I should see my dentist, but I also knew that in treating the tooth he might cause me more pain. So there was the temptation to endure the toothache rather than face the dentist. So with other suffering. We gradually become accustomed to the pain and prefer to keep it rather than accept the pain of positive action and remedy.

Gradually, we become negative in our thinking. Instead of concentrating on our blessings, we fill our minds with our woes. We fail to see the blue sky and bright sunshine because our eyes are focused on some cloud on the horizon. Trouble comes, and, little by little, it takes possession of our entire thought processes. Our whole life revolves around that trouble.

When that happens, we become constant complainers. We cannot talk about the blessings and beauties of life, because we do not see them. We cannot gain inspiration and courage from our dreams and hopes, because our misery has destroyed them. So we can only complain. Before long, our complaints get worse than our troubles and then we artificially keep our troubles alive, nurture them, and even manufacture new troubles to keep up with our complaints.

Thus a person gets into a descending spiral of defeat and misery.

However, there is a better way. I had dinner recently in another city in one of the loveliest homes it has been my privilege to visit. The house and furnishings were beautiful, but there was something more. There was a spirit of gentleness and kindness in that home one seldom meets. The husband and wife are both making a marvelous contribution to the cultural and spiritual life of their community.

Later, I learned the complete story. This couple had only one child. Physically, he is perfect, but his mind has never developed. He is now a twenty-year-old boy with the mind of a baby, and is kept in an institution. But instead of the tragedy making the parents bitter, it has served to make them better.

Jesus took the cross of sin and made it the cure for sin; He took the hate of man and made it the revelation of God's love; He took the harshest word of man and made it God's tenderest utterance. Jesus did not merely bear the cross; He used it for the salvation of the world. He turned sorrow into a song, Calvary into Easter. He is our example.

I have known very few conceited people. Many give that impression, but most of the time the appearance of conceit is a mask one wears to hide a feeling of inferiority. The most common fear people have is the fear of being their real self. For those who feel inferior I would like to make some helpful suggestions.

First, find out exactly why you have a feeling of inferiority. It may be some physical handicap. Remember St. Paul's "thorn in the flesh." We do not know what it was, but it is thought to have been some physical limitation. As you study his writings, you see that it gave him great concern over his ability to fulfill his duties and responsibilities.

Or it may be some experience you had in childhood. Recently I talked with a man who had a morbid fear because of his own inabilities. We discovered that when he was a boy in school he barely made passing grades, while his older brother made A's. His parents, in a misguided effort to stimulate him, constantly held before him the fact that his brother did so well while he did so poorly. The continued taunting nearly wrecked his life.

Perhaps somewhere along the way you made a mistake and it so embarrassed you that you have never quite overcome it. A man told me of his deep longing to be able to make a speech, but when a child in school he was to say a piece, and forgot it. Everybody laughed, and he has never been able to try it again.

Sometimes people feel inferior because there is something on their conscience. Nothing makes a coward out of a person quicker than sin. "The wicked flee when no man pursueth; but the righteous are as bold as a lion" (Proverbs 28:1).

If you feel inferior, there is a cause. Go back over your life; find the cause and face it honestly. That is the first step.

Second, analyze your abilities. You cannot do everything that others can do, but there is something that you can accomplish. Decide what it is, and concentrate on it rather than worry about the things you cannot do.

When I started out as a preacher, I had very small churches and I did almost everything. I preached the sermons, did all the visiting, acted as secretary, and answered all the calls made on my time.

Now I find myself in a different position. In a large church no one person can do it all. I worried about the visits I could not make, all the opportunities of service I had to turn down. Then one day I sat down and decided what I could do, and arranged a program and a schedule. I am much happier because of it.

There is something you can do. What is it?

Third, do not quit because you have failed. There was a man who wanted to be a writer. Particularly did he want to write stories for the movies. He wrote one on the life of John Paul Jones and sent it to Miss Julia West, story editor of Paramount Pictures. She had to reject it.

Later he told her of his bitter disappointment. But he said that the rejection taught him that a failure, no matter how dismal it may make the future seem, doesn't mean the end of a man's life. He said he learned that the best way to overcome failure is to put it in the past and go on with the determination to succeed.

That man was Franklin D. Roosevelt.

Fourth, think success instead of failure. It is one of the fundamental laws of life that one tends to become what he pictures himself to be.

All too often we are like the ten spies who went into the Promised Land. They saw that the land was good, but they also saw giants in the way. They concentrated on the obstacles instead of on the goal, and they failed.

Finally, realize that there is power available to help you. It is the power of God. Use the "ten-word cure" for inferiority. It is, "If God be for me, who can be against me?" Repeat that slowly and confidently every time you feel the need of it.

In the third chapter of Acts, there is a story in ten short verses that would take a modern novelist several hundred pages to write. Peter and John were on their way to church. It was a strange pair. John—one of the Sons of Thunder—was vehement, zealous, intense. He was the first to recognize the risen Lord on the shore of Tiberias.

Peter was impetuous and changeable. He talked big, but many times had failed to live up to his talk. He started a lot of things he could not carry out. But a marvelous change had come into the lives of both these men.

On the steps of the church sat a beggar who had been lame all his life. Every day he would sit there with his dirty, pitiful hand stretched out, begging for alms in a whining tone. Probably for many years people had given to him, yet that had not solved his problem. His problem was not one of money but of inner defeat.

Peter did not give money to the beggar. For one thing, he had none to give. Another reason is that Peter, because of what had happened to him, knew that the man needed more than money. As you read the story, watch Peter's technique. It is marvelous.

First, he looked straight at the man. The story says, "And Peter, fastening his eyes upon him . . ." There is tremendous power in eye concentration. Peter then commanded, "Look on us." The beggar probably had reached the point where he did not like to look other people in the eye. But there was something in Peter's voice that made him look up. Slowly and painfully, his weak, watery eyes met Peter's level gaze.

He looked into a face that was weather-beaten and roughened by many years at sea. Yet it was a face that was solid, like a granite cliff. On it was a glow, a glow reflected from a light shining within. The beggar's attention was captured and held by the sheer magnetism of this man Peter.

Slowly, Peter began talking, the words falling from his lips like the sure, heavy blows of a sledge hammer. You must read between the lines here to get Peter's words, but they went something like this:

"I used to be defeated too. But one day Jesus said, 'Come ye after me and I will make you.' Through contact and association with Him, I found new strength and power. I am today a changed man. Not only did He 'make' John and me, he made blind men see, sick people well, and crippled people—people just like you—walk."

Here he is building up the man's hopes and faith. He is using a basic law of science—what has been done can be done. If Christ could do what He had done for John and Peter and many others, He could also do it for even a lame beggar.

It is quite possible that this beggar did not want to hear about the possibility of a cure. Many people think they hate their chains, and they pray for freedom. Yet, actually, they do not want to be free.

Recently I talked with a young man who is sick. But his sickness is in his mind rather than in his body, as he believes. He came to me, but, really, he did not want my help. He wanted my sympathy, not my help. His sickness is a crutch, and he enjoys leaning on it. It is an escape for him, because he is afraid to stand on his feet and be a real man.

But Peter knew of a power that can lift even a lame man who has let his lameness get into his mind. It was not mere psychology. He did not say, "Think you walk and you can." That would have been enough. Notice carefully Peter's words, "In the name of Jesus Christ of Nazareth rise up and walk."

There is a power available to man far greater than mere human power. Strength began to flow into the lame man's ankle bones. He stood on his feet without falling, then he began to walk, then to leap, and then to praise God. I cannot explain it any better than a physician can explain the X-ray, but during nearly two thousand years, whenever men put faith in Jesus Christ marvelous changes have come into their lives.

The Big Question of Forgiveness

THIS IS A story of a man who committed adultery, broke up a home and, indirectly, committed murder. He was a very unusual man, in fact, one of the greatest men of all time. While he was still a very young man he visited his brothers in the army. That day he saw a giant of the enemy stand on a hill and challenge any one to fight him. But all were afraid to face the giant.

However, David was not afraid and he asked Saul to let him fight. He told Saul how that, as he watched over the sheep, he fought a bear and a lion and God took care of him. Saul let him go and Goliath laughed as he saw the boy coming out to fight. But David said, "Thou comest to me with a sword, and with a spear, and with a shield: but I come to thee in the name of the Lord" (1 Samuel 17:45). He killed the giant.

As David grew, he studied and worked. He became one of the greatest musicians of his day, he wrote poetry that will live forever, he was a scholar of first rank. One of the finest stories of the Bible is that of his friendship with Jonathan. He later became an astute statesman. In every sense he was a great, a good, and a deeply spiritual man.

He became a general in Saul's army and, after a great victory over the Philistines, he was given a hero's welcome back home. Crowds lined the streets, shouting, "Saul hath slain his thousands, and David his ten thousands" (I Samuel 18:7). Saul could not stand that comparison and, in his jealous rage, set out to kill David. David fled for his life, and Saul and his men set out to hunt him down.

Though he was wronged, David kept the right spirit. One night Saul and his men slept in a cave in which David was hiding. He slipped out and cut off a piece of Saul's shirt while he slept. Another time David crept into Saul's camp and stuck a spear into the ground by the head of the sleeping Saul. He was showing Saul he could have killed him, but was unwilling to return hate for hate.

At length, Saul died, and David became king. Israel never had a greater king than he. The first thing he did was to arrange for and encourage divine worship. He knew that no nation could become great without God. He united the twelve tribes into a solid nation, built roads and developed commerce that brought prosperity to his people. He made treaties that brought peace.

Then is when it happened. Not when he was struggling or fighting or working. But when he became strong and secure. He saw a woman whom he liked. He entertained wicked thoughts, and, step by step, he let himself get out of hand. He broke up her home, put her husband in a position to be killed, and began to live in sin.

Then, one day, his preacher, Nathan, came to see him. Nathan told the king a story about a rich man who had many flocks. One day he had a guest and, instead of killing one of his own sheep for the guest, he took the only lamb of a poor man and killed that. David was upset over the story. Then the preacher shook his finger in the king's face, and shouted, "Thou art the man."

David might have cut the preacher's head off, or quit the church, but, instead, his cheeks went white, his knees began to tremble, and he began to pray. He prayed just the prayer that an adulterer and murderer should pray. And it is just the prayer for a sinner like you and me to pray. His prayer is the 51st Psalm.

He humbly confesses his sin. He offers no excuses, pleads no mitigating circumstances, blames nobody else. Then he asks for God's mercy, and prays, "Create within me a clean heart, O God." He then vows a new consecration.

Did God hear, forgive and restore him? In my experience as pastor of a church in a big city, men and women have come to my study time and again with the terrible burden of a guilt complex. Many felt that there was no hope for them, that they were forever cut off from God. I told them about David and the steps he took—confession, putting their faith in God's forgiving mercy, turning completely away from the wrong they had committed and consecrating their life thenceforth.

Do those steps really work? I would then turn and read the 23rd Psalm. David wrote that Psalm long years after his act of adultery, and with joy in his heart he said, "He leadeth me beside the still waters. He restoreth my soul. . . . I will fear no evil. . . . And I will dwell in the house of the Lord forever."

The reason we have churches and preachers is not to condemn people who have missed the way, but to point the way back to peace, to happiness, and to salvation.

A number of people have talked to me who were afraid they had committed the unpardonable sin. Certainly there is such a sin. Jesus says: "Whosoever speaketh against the Holy Ghost, it shall not be forgiven him, neither in this world, neither in the world to come." (Read Matthew 12:31,32 and Mark 3:28,29.)

First, let me say two things about the unpardonable sin: (1) It is not some particular sin. Some people have felt that if you broke one of the Ten Commandments, that was unpardonable. But remember that David broke several of them and was forgiven.

Second, if you have any worry or fears that you have committed the unforgivable sin, it is a sure sign that you have not. Those who are guilty of this sin never so much as give it a thought, much less worry about it.

Now let us see exactly what this sin is. When a person does wrong it hurts his conscience. That is the Holy Spirit at work on that person. But, later, that person can do the same thing again and his conscience will hurt a little less. Finally he becomes so habituated to committing the wrongful act that he never gives it a thought or feels any remorse.

A similar thing happens in many areas of a life. I have known people who had reached the point where they had no appreciation for beauty. There are people who do not respond to music. Other people become so completely selfish that they cannot love another person.

It is a law of life that you will eventually lose those

of your powers you do not use. There are rivers in the Mammoth Cave in Kentucky that flow in total darkness. Fish in those rivers have eyes but cannot see because the faculty of sight has never been used.

So with one's ability to respond to God's Spirit. God comes through His Spirit to every person, and points out certain duties and responsibilities, or rebukes us for certain wrongs we do.

But a person can turn a deaf ear to the voice of God so long that eventually he is unable to respond. In the parable of the sower (Matthew 13:3-9) Jesus tells us that it is possible for a heart to become so hardened that the seed of God cannot take root in it at all.

It isn't that God refuses to pardon sin. God will always pardon. But pardon is a two-way proposition. Man must also be willing and able to receive pardon. And one can say no to the voice of God so often that he cannot say yes.

There are five stages in human activity and development. (1) Volition, which is simply the free exercise of your will. Any man can decide to do wrong or to do right. God gave us that power.

(2) An act. When you decide, the carrying out of the decision is an act.

(3) Habit. One keeps making the same decisions over and over and repeating the same acts until they become a habit. More than we realize, our lives are made up of hundreds of habits we have developed.

(4) Character. Your character is you, and you are what you think and do. A baby has no character when it

is born, but immediately begins forming its pattern of life.

Character may become fixed so that if one forms a completely Godless character he has nothing within him to respond to the voice of God's Spirit. Such a person does not hear the voice because his soul has become paralyzed or atrophied.

(5) The final stage is your eternal destiny, which is determined by your character.

To sum up: One has committed the unpardonable sin when, because of continued indifference to God and continuance of evil habits, he forms a Godless character and becomes incapable of hearing or responding to God's Spirit.

A person came to me with this question, "Will God answer my prayers if I have done wrong?" I turned to Psalm 66:18 and read, "If I regard iniquity in my heart, the Lord will not hear me."

Then I asked, "What wrong have you done?" He replied, "Lots of things." I said, "You did not come to me because you are bothered about 'lots of things.' You are bothered about some specific thing. If we can settle that *one* thing, then the 'lots of things' will be easy to handle."

I like to hunt quail, but I am a very poor shot. A friend once told me the reason. When a covey of quail rises, I shoot at all of them. That is wrong. Regardless of how many birds there are, I should pick out one, get it clearly in my sights and then pull the trigger.

A friend was suffering terribly. His knees hurt. He had pains in his back, even his feet were sore. He wanted me to pray for him, and I did, but I also insisted that he have a complete examination by his physician. The physician decided it might be his teeth and sent him to a dentist. The dentist x-rayed the teeth and found one badly abscessed. When that one source of infection was eliminated, the pains in his body were eliminated.

I was preaching in a series of revival services on this theme, when, at the close of the sermon, the song leader sang that familiar chorus, "I surrender all, I surrender all." He sang it with deep feeling. He said that song meant everything to him now, but that there had been a time when it disturbed him greatly. Then he had sung, "I surrender all (except one thing), I surrender all (except one thing)." But one day he honestly faced and surrendered that one thing, and joy and peace came flooding into his life.

Many people worry about past mistakes and failures. That is a worry that nothing can heal. But when we get down to specific cases it is amazing how quickly they can be settled.

A woman was quite worried over the fact that she seemed not to be able to get along with people. It seemed that nobody loved her and everybody was against her. I suggested that she name one person in particular. She named her husband's sister.

We began talking about why she and her sister-in-law could not get along with each other and what she might do to bring about a reconciliation so that each could have the complete confidence and friendship of the other. It was easy to talk about this specific case and point out concrete methods or procedure.

We settled on a plan for her to follow with her sister-in-law. She was to concentrate on it until her aim was accomplished. Then we were to take up some other cases. But she told me later that since she and her sister-in-law had worked out their differences and become fast friends, it seemed that she was now getting along all right with everybody else. It usually works out that way.

Instead of worrying about getting along with people, pick out one person you like the least and who irritates you the most, and concentrate on him. Then decide on a specific plan of action to become his friend and make him yours. It is amazing how that one experience will influence your feelings toward all other people and their feelings toward you.

Or, if you have a guilty conscience because of "lots of things," sit down quietly and deliberately decide definitely what was one thing you have done that was wrong. You should write it down.

Then honestly ask yourself what you can do about it. Perhaps then you can make some restitution. Maybe nothing can be done about it now. But whatever the cost, settle that one thing with God and your own conscience.

When you have done what you can about it and have asked the forgiveness of God and your own forgiveness, then burn up the slip of paper on which you had written your error and remember it no more. It will thrill your heart to discover how easy it is to settle the "lots of things" after that one thing is out of the way.

The most divinely tender and humanly touching story ever told on earth is the story Jesus told us of the father welcoming home his wayward boy. We call it the story of "The Prodigal Son." But really it should be called the story of "The Forgiving Father." Jesus told it to reveal God's attitude to us when we have done wrong (Luke 15:11-24).

In this story Jesus leads up to the grand climax of the father's love by the staircase of the boy's life. (1) There is self-will. "Give me. . . . The younger son gathered all together and took his journey into a far country."

Home was irksome. The young man wanted freedom. He was tired of the rules and restraints of the father. He wanted to live his life as he pleased. The father made no attempt to hold him. Had the father held the boy against his will, home would have become a prison and the father a jailer.

The Pharisees set up an elaborate system of laws and regulations and attempted to force people to accept them. Not so with the religion of Christ. He shows us the way, but it is entirely a voluntary matter whether or not one follows that way. If we wish we can choose some other way with perfect freedom.

(2) The second step is *always* the second step: "He began to be in want." His once radiant spirit becomes as bedraggled as his clothes. One can live away from God and never want for material things. We see that demonstrated again and again. But there is a deeper and more real want. It is the longing of one's heart, the thirst of one's soul in the far country away from God.

In an effort to satisfy his wants "he went and joined himself to a citizen of that country and he sent him into the fields to feed swine." Note carefully that word "sent." Now where is his boasted freedom? He who lives to do as he likes eventually becomes the slave of his likes. Someone has well said, "No one ever breaks the laws of God. He breaks himself instead of the laws."

(3) "And when he came to himself" is the third step. No man is a single self. There is our passionate self, which, when it gives way to such passions as fear, lust, hate, etc., controls our thinking and actions, and brings us down to the level of beasts. There is our greedy self, which gives no thought to the rights and feelings of others. And there is our careless self, which just drifts along without bothering to think.

And then there is our best self, the self that Shakespeare meant when he said, "To thine own self be true." We sometimes say, "I was not myself," which is an exact expression. When, in the far country, he looked into the face of a hog and realized the level to which he had sunk, that prodigal boy knew he was not himself.

(4) Not from outer compulsion but from an inner awakening, he now takes the fourth step, "Father I have sinned. . . . Make me . . ." There is the key that unlocks the door of home. Without it no one can ever re-enter. There is no pardoning mercy even from the Father of mercy until we repent. There is no forgiveness possible for one who feels no need of repentance.

One definition of repentance is to change one's mind in regard to one's conduct. The experience of repentance comes when one becomes convinced that his way has been the wrong way, when he is genuinely sorry for his sin, sorry to the point where he is willing to keep forever from his evil way, no matter what the cost.

And so the boy says, "Make me as one of thy hired servants." He realizes he is not quite as big as he thought he was. Before, he was saying, "Give me . . ." but now he realizes that it is not what he can get from the father that is important, but rather is it what the father can do for him and through him that counts. So with God. God pours His blessings freely on the just and the unjust. But when we let Him, God will work in us and through us a high purpose in life.

(5) Now comes the main step, "When he was yet a great way off, his father saw him, and had compassion, and ran, and fell on his neck, and kissed him," and restored him. No period of waiting, no sharp reproof. The forgiveness is complete.

The loving forgiveness of God is what makes life bearable. In the lives of most of us there is a shameful chapter. We can take the way of Judas or the way of Simon Peter. Both sinned, and neither could bear his sin. Judas went out and hanged himself, but Peter came back to Christ. The old song is ever new and ever needed. "He breaks the power of canceled sin, He sets the prisoner free; His blood can make the foulest clean; His blood availed for me."

Following is the first sermon I ever preached. It is the Christian Gospel as I see it:

A girl I know had been an orphan all her life. Her mother had died. Her father had disappeared, and he was presumed to be dead. She never knew what it meant to be really loved by anybody. She was very lonely and love-starved.

Through the years, her father had become a very successful and famous man but he, too, was unhappy. He knew that somewhere there was a lovely girl who was his daughter, and his one hope in life was to find her. The years slipped by and, after nearly twenty years of searching, he was about to give her up as lost.

Then one day the father received a bit of information that brought hope to his heart. He dropped everything to follow this new lead. There was a girl living in Atlanta who might be his daughter. Before he let her know anything, he carefully checked and joyously he discovered she really was his own daughter.

One day a big, fine man drove up in an elegant car before a cheap boarding house. He asked for this girl, and when she came to the door he said, "I am your father and I have come to take you home." He showed her the proof, and she knew it was true. She says, "No one can ever know what it meant to me when I discovered that I had a father."

Out of the boarding house she moved to live in a lovely home. What a glorious transformation she experienced in her life.

For thousands of years the people had believed in a God, but he was stern, vengeful and cold. He demanded sacrifices and exacted justice. He was a God who thundered repentance, who was fearful in his judgments, and who was stern and unapproachable.

Then Jesus came, says St. Mark, preaching "God's good news" (1:14) (Weymouth). The purpose of that Babe being born in Bethlehem was to tell people that we have a Father. Instead of burnt offerings, He taught us to pray, "Our Father." Instead of a God of punishment, the children of earth were told of One who loves with an eternal love.

Ian Maclaren gave us the story of Latchland Campbell. He was a Pharisee, stern and cold. He loved his daughter Flora, but her mother had died and because her father was so lacking in compassion and understanding, Flora ran away from home.

Rumors started coming back of the sinful life Flora had fallen into, and one day Latchland struck her name from the record in the family Bible. The next Sunday he made the motion at church that her name be dropped from the roll. The congregation refused, however, to take action without further study.

The next week Margie Howe, a kind lady, went to see Latchland. She told him the story of the prodigal son and the father. He finally consented for Margie to write to Flora. So Margie wrote: "Lassie, come home, for your old father is a-grieving for you. Come home for your sake. Come home for your father's sake, and come home for the dear Lord's sake."

Flora was sick in body and in heart when she received that letter, and she came immediately. The next week Margie Howe came to call again. There was the old family Bible on the table opened to the family record page. In the writing of a trembling old man were these words: "Flora Campbell, she went away in May but she came back in December and her father fell upon her neck and kissed her."

"In my Father's house are many mansions," and, no matter who you are or what you have done, the Father loves you and wants you to come home. That is His message.

In Arnold Bennett's diary you do not find very many exciting entries, but there is one I think is wonderful. It is this: "John Buchan, invited for tea at 4:30, arrived at 4:27. And at 5:15, he simply got up and left."

"He simply got up and left"—what a thrilling word that is. A man who knew how to leave. We all have callers who stay on and on and on. You try every method you have ever heard of to get rid of them but nothing works.

A friend of mine has suggested that a sure-fire method of getting rid of people who do not know how to leave is to ask the guest to have some refreshments and serve him a glass containing one part coco-cola and two parts tabasco sauce. I have never tried that, but admit I have been tempted.

Knowing how and when to leave is one of the most important lessons one can learn. For example, there was Lot's wife. She lived in Sodom, but Sodom was about to be destroyed. The Lord told Lot and his wife that they would be saved if they would flee the city without looking back. They started out, but poor Mrs. Lot had not learned how to leave. So she stopped to look back, and was changed into a pillar of salt.

A man told me recently how unhappy he is in his marriage. He has a lovely wife and he loves her, but he cannot forget some of the other girls he used to go with, and he wonders what life would have been like with them. He married the girl he wanted most, but in his mind he has never been able to give up the other girls completely.

In talking about marriage, Jesus says: "For this cause shall a man leave his father and mother, and cleave to his wife." So long as one lives, he owes a debt to his parents, but there is a sense in which one must leave his parents when he marries. Unless this rule is followed marriages usually do not work out very well. And there is the obligation on the parents to let the child leave.

In every large city there are thousands of people who are very unhappy simply because they have never learned how to leave the old home town. Recently, a woman asked me for help. I inquired who her pastor was. She explained that she loved the little church back home so much that she just could not change her membership. I asked her how long it had been since she had attended the dear old church, and she told me it had been fourteen years.

During those fourteen years she really had had no church, simply because she did not know how to leave.

Dr. Pierce Harris tells of an old ship captain who said: "Even if I am in port for only one day I let my anchor down."

Some people never learn to leave the "good old days." They live in the past and miss all the thrilling opportunities of a day like this. Jesus once said: "No man, having put his hand to the plow, and looking back, is fit for the kingdom of God" (Luke 9:62). He means that we are to keep our eyes forward, leaving the past in the sense that it should not hold and control us.

Many people never learn to leave their sorrows. For example, it is a tragic experience to have a child die. But it is a much greater tragedy for a father and mother to quit living because of the sorrow.

I conduct many funerals, each of which seems the saddest. But I believe that the saddest of all is to see a couple separated who have walked happily down life's pathways together.

Not long ago I had a chance to talk with Mrs. Billy Sunday. She is one of the greatest Christians I know. Now, at the age of eighty-three, she is doing a great work. She told me that when her famous husband died, instead of being bitter, she got on her knees and prayed, "Here I am, Lord. Use me in any way you like." She knew how to leave a sorrow and go on.

Finally, there is great need to learn how to leave our sins. David besought God, to blot out his transgressions

(Psalm 51:1). And God does do that for all of us when we rightly ask. He remembers our sins against us no more. Yet, after He forgives them, many people never learn to forgive themselves. They carry the weight of some past sin the balance of their days.

"He simply got up and left." May his tribe increase!

Take Time for God

WE AMERICANS HAVE the most comfortable homes ever built, the finest beds ever made, luxurious automobiles in which to ride, the most elaborate recreational facilities of all time, and the shortest work week in our history. Yet the fact is, we are a tired and weary people.

Dante, the Italian poet, when asked by some monks where he was going and what he was seeking, replied, "I am searching for that which every man seeks—peace and rest." And, as we go into a new year, most of us have that same desire deep in our hearts.

We have lofty ambitions, which we struggle to accomplish. We want to get ahead, to excell, to make a big contribution to the world. Yet there are conflicting desires in our hearts. We would like to have a little cabin out in the woods, smell the pines, and hear the soft rustle of the wind through the trees.

It would be good to have a little stream running near by and listen to the gentle splashing of the water over the rocks. A log fire would be nice, and a big rocking chair in which to rock slowly as we watch the red coals turn to grey would be so cozy and comfortable.

A popular magazine stated recently: "Business men who are constantly tired may be on the verge of a breakdown. An examination of over two thousand tired business men by Philadelphia's Franklin Clinic found many suffering from hypertension. Cure: Relaxation."

After Mr. John C. Winant, former governor of his state and wartime ambassador to Great Britain, had taken his life, an editorial writer said of him: "He was a tired man. He went back to New Hampshire to rest, but unhappily he had forgotten how to rest." And that is a pretty good commentary on the American way of life.

For most of us, the little cabin in the woods where we can "get away from it all" is not possible. But we can learn how to rest. First, we must remember that tiredness has various causes. There is a delicious tiredness that results from eighteen holes of golf or an honest and productive day's work. I have never known of anyone working himself to death.

The tiredness that robs life of all joy is the result of something we plan for the future. To overcome that I think of three references in the wisest book on how to live that has ever been written.

Moses had on his shoulders a big and very difficult job. It would require all his strength and more, and he was very hesitant about undertaking it. He would have much preferred to quietly watch his sheep as he had been doing. But God assured him with these words: "My presence shall go with thee, and I will give thee rest" (Exodus 33:14).

Once Jesus looked out on a group of people just like we are today, and He said: "Come unto me, all ye that labor and are heavy laden, and I will give you rest. . . . Take my yoke upon you . . . and ye shall find rest unto your souls" (Matthew 11:28,29).

Just before His ascension, Jesus had talked to His followers about conquering the world in His name. It was an almost impossible task, but He told them: "Tarry ye in the city of Jerusalem, until ye be endued with power from on high" (Luke 24:49).

Tiredness breaks us because we set high standards of accomplishment for ourselves and then feel that we lack the resources to reach them. And the inner conflict that results puts a heavy strain on us.

But, when one realizes that he has resources beyond his own—the resources of Almighty God—his mind is relieved of stress and strain and relaxes.

Dr. Stanley Jones once had a nervous breakdown. His doctors said he was doing too much and that he must give up much of his work. He was flat on his back, but he said he heard God speaking to him even as He had spoken to Moses, "My presence will go with thee, and I will give thee rest." He believed that and went back to work. He took as the motto of his life: "Let go and let God." Today he is doing even more than ever before and is in perfect health.

Jesus never ran. Peter and John ran, Paul and Barnabas ran, Philip ran, the multitudes about Jesus ran, but He never ran. He was tremendously busy. He had a big job to do and only three years to work at it, but He was never in a hurry.

He went to parties and had time for people. As He walked along through life he saw the flowers and the birds. He would turn aside and take time for little children. He would take a day or two off and go into the mountains to meditate, rest, and pray. He would get in a boat and go out on the sea.

If there is one lesson this generation needs to learn, it is how to take time to live. I enjoy watching people in church. Many sit as if they think the pew might fall down. They fret if there is any lost time during the service. They want the service to be short and snappy, and the minute the benediction is pronounced they break for the door like a bunch of motorcycles taking off when a red light has turned to green.

I talk privately with a lot of people, most of whom start the interview by saying "I know you are in a hurry." But long ago I learned you cannot counsel with people on the run. I tell many that they have already run past far more than they will ever catch up with.

I sometimes feel I would like to belong to the old-fashioned Quaker Church. The modern Quakers have preachers, but the old ones would just "go to meeting." Now, if the spirit moves one to get up and talk, he does, but otherwise they just sit quietly to think and pray.

Someone has beautifully said: "I know a peace where there is no peace, a calm where the wild winds blow. A secret place where, face to face with the Master, I may go." The person who has that is rich indeed.

God says, "Be still, and know that I am God" (Psalm 46:10). One reason so many people today have no sense of the presence of God is that they have been running too hard.

A friend of mine tells of driving with his family

through the mountains of North Carolina. Along the highway were signs, reading, "The Land of the Sky." Reading these signs, his little boy asked, "Daddy, does God live here?" "Yes, son," the father replied, "God lives everywhere."

As they drove along, they passed an old man with a flowing white beard and a long staff. The little boy excitedly shouted, "Look daddy, I see God." And as the father looked around at these mountains, he said, "Yes, son, I see God, too." Many people who are not in a hurry have learned to say with the Psalmist, "The heavens declare the glory of God; and the firmament showeth his handiwork" (Psalm 19:1).

As a minister, some of my finest hours have been with people who are sick. Before, they had been so hurried and active, but sickness came, and they were in bed for a period of enforced stillness. God sometimes puts one on his back so that he can look up. I know many people who in sickness found the answers they had sought. Not because they were afraid of dying, but rather because they were still for a while.

Nearly every week I am in a home where death has come. In such a time there are so many things to see about. People crowd in, and the strain is often very heavy. I always advise the loved ones whose hearts have been hurt to shut themselves away for some time alone with their sorrow. Again and again, people have said to me later that God became more real to them in that quiet time than He had ever been before.

For many years God had tried to break into the life of St. Paul. But He could never enter until Paul took that trip to Damascus. Paul was too busy. But a few days before, Paul had seen Stephen stoned. As he slowly rode along through the desert to Damascus, he began to realize that somewhere along the way he had missed what Stephen had. And he saw a vision that forever changed his life.

One week I was on a train for three days. I went from Atlanta to New York to Chicago and back to Atlanta. I had a private bedroom all the way. There was no telephone and there were no people. I had time to think about what God has done for me, about my work and my opportunities, and as I said my prayers at night it was easier to resolve to be more thankful and more faithful.

Jesus never ran.

In Panama City, Florida, for a week's revival, I had a hotel room overlooking the great Gulf of Mexico. It was a stimulating experience, and while there I thought of a great prescription that a very wise physician gave a patient. He told him to "get off and look at something big."

Jesus often would slip away from the crowds, get in a boat and go out to sea. He would go up to the mountains to pray and meditate. Surely one of His favorite quotations was: "I will lift up mine eyes unto the hills, from whence cometh my help" (Psalm 121:1).

When you see something big, it lifts you out of yourself. I get a great blessing every time I see Stone Mountain. It is so strong and sturdy that it gives assurance that everything is not falling to pieces.

The very life that many city people live makes for instability. We get up in the morning and eat a bite of breakfast on the run. We hurry to catch a bus and crowd our way in, frequently having to stand all the way to the office. If we drive we fret over the heavy traffic and worry about a place to park.

Many work all day in a dull, unimaginative office at routine jobs. We choke down a sandwich at lunch, often standing at a counter. We crowd our way home at night, too tired and irritable to enjoy dinner. Finally, we go to bed facing the same thing tomorrow.

There is no time to dream and to build ideals. It is so easy to become blinded to the fact there is anything big, and one drifts into thinking what Bertrand Russell expressed: "Brief and powerless is man's life. On him and all his race the slow, sure doom falls pitiless and dark." A sort of "what's-the-use-of-living" despondency.

A slight pain in my foot had persisted for two or three days, and I phoned a doctor about looking at it. He suggested that I come by his home the next morning about ten o'clock. When I arrived he was sitting in a beautiful den before a log fire.

He told me that sometimes he doesn't go to his office until noon. Instead, he sits there before the fire and thinks about things. He pulled up a big chair for me and we chatted a while. He talked about spending an entire day and night in a fox-hole during the last war. There was nothing he could do and any minute might be his last.

He lay there thinking of the war and of life and what a man is supposed to get out of living. He said it is true that "there are no atheists in fox-holes." He thought about God and the way he had treated Him. He resolved to live differently and better.

After I left, I realized that he had not looked at my

foot. He forgot it and I did, too. But the pain had gone and I have not felt it since. Maybe the warmth of the fire cured it. Maybe just forgetting it and thinking about more important things was the cure. Anyway, the doctor's life was changed one day when he was away and saw something big.

A thrilling new book is Mr. J. C. Penney's autobiography, *Fifty Years with the Golden Rule.* In it he tells of being in a sanitarium one night when he thought he was dying. He wrote several letters and went back to bed thinking he would not be alive the next morning. But he was alive when morning came.

He got up and as he was walking down the hall he heard some people singing: "Be not dismayed whate'er betide. God will take care of you." It was a few people having an early morning prayer meeting, and he slipped in and sat in a seat at the back.

Quietly someone read from the Bible, and lead in prayer. Mr. Penney spontaneously said, "Lord, I can do nothing. Will you take care of me?" He says: "In the next few moments something happened to me. . . . It was a miracle."

He saw something big in that little prayer meeting. It saved him. Many others see it in church on Sunday.

One of the profoundest thinkers America has ever produced was Ralph Waldo Emerson. He said, "Neither you nor the world knows what you can do until you have tried." I am constantly amazed at the number of people who never have really tried. A lot of people make a start, but quit before they give themselves a real chance.

In the 27th Psalm (v. 13), the Psalmist says, "I had

fainted, unless . . ." He is saying that he almost quit and would have quit except for the fact that he believed in God. He begins the Psalm by saying, "The Lord is my light and my salvation; whom shall I fear?"

In the first place, faith in God always gives one faith in himself. When people lack self-confidence they do crazy things. Some become the dictator type. They boast and brag, swagger and strut, and seek to dominate everybody they can.

Others who feel inferior try to overcome it by retreating into a world of daydreams. Not willing to face life as it really is, they create illusions within their minds. Such a course often causes inner conflicts and can even lead to a split personality.

Then, some people are like the fox in Aesop's fable. Because he could not reach the grapes, he said they were sour and not worth reaching. One of the surest signs that a person lacks faith in himself is criticism and belittling the accomplishments of others.

But when one puts his faith in a personal God there comes surging into his life a wonderful strength. "The Lord is the strength of my life," the Psalmist says. That gives a person the nerve to try.

In the second place, the Psalmist had lost confidence in other people. He has a great deal to say about his enemies. He was suspicious and afraid of people. That is enough to take the heart out of anybody.

A man who had lost a leg in an accident said he wanted to give up, but his wife kept saying, "Don't you worry. I will always stay with you, and whatever walking you cannot do I will do for you." His faith in her and her faith in him is what kept him going.

In the fourth century there lived Athanasius, a great theologian. His principles were so unpopular at the time that there arose a saying, "Athanasius against the world." He never wavered in his stand, but I dare say had one looked behind the scenes he would have found a small group of loyal friends whose love and loyalty gave him the strength that he needed.

I spend a lot of time out of town preaching in other churches. The people provide me with the best hotel rooms available, invite me into lovely homes for fine dinners, give me a chance to speak to large crowds, and are most generous in every way.

But I would never be willing to be a full-time traveling evangelist. I want my own congregation. I want to be with people who know me, who believe in me and to whom I belong. No matter how noisy the children get, it is still better to be at home among your very own. Without the backing of some who love you, life is almost impossible.

Usually, the reason one loses faith in others is because he has developed no faith inside himself. Faith begets faith, and when the Psalmist put his faith in God, faith in his fellow man naturally came, as did their faith in him.

Third, the Psalmist says the thing that kept him trying was that he believed that, somehow, things would work out all right. "I had fainted," he says, "unless I had believed to see the goodness of the Lord in the land of the living" (27:13).

Archibald Rutledge tells about a trip he took in a

tiny tugboat. In the doorway of the engine room he saw a Negro reading his Bible. The Negro was immaculately clean. The engine room behind him was spotless.

When Mr. Rutledge inquired how he managed to keep everything so clean, the Negro replied, "Cap'n, its jest thisa way. I'se got a glory." Mr. Rutledge said, "Having a glory he had everything."

The Psalmist did not faint because believing in God gave him a glory. Because of his confidence in himself and others and the assurance that tomorrow would be better, he tried and kept on trying.

"Why do preachers dig up those old characters in the Bible and talk about them? I am interested in people and life today." That is a good question that came in a recent letter and the answer is simply that, while nearly everything else has changed, people are the same today as they were several thousand years ago.

God has not changed, and the relation of man to God and God to man is the same today as ever before. Thus, the fundamental problems of people today are the same as they always have been. You can study a mountain better from a distance and you can also study human life and behavior better from a distance. We know Abraham Lincoln today better than he was known in his lifetime.

So with our Bible characters, who were the great people of their generations. Take the prophet Jeremiah, for example. Recently I have been restudying his life, and I find he was about like people today. He was a man of the same moods that I see in many whom I counsel.

Jeremiah had his tearful moods. In fact, he has been called the "weeping prophet." He once said, "I wish I could just cry my eyes out." Many people have crying moods. Shelley said, "I feel like a tired child, and could sit down and cry my life away." St. Paul tells us that tears often rolled down his cheeks. We remember that Jesus wept.

Jeremiah had his moods of disgust. He said, "O that I had in the wilderness a lodging place that I might leave my people and go from them." He had those moments when he felt there was no use trying any longer. He just wanted to run away from it all.

He also had his cynical moods. He grew up in a little village and later, when he came to the city, very soon somebody tried to cheat him. So he drew the conclusion that everybody in the city was out to cheat and swindle. He became cynical about people.

Jeremiah also had his vindictive moods. Once Pashur, an official of the temple, put him in stocks and left him there all day and night. Some of the things he said were terrible. One day he was so angry with the people that he actually prayed that their children would starve to death. He prayed that their men might be killed in battle. He even begged God not to forgive their sins.

He had his moods of depression. At times he became so depressed that he cursed the day he was born. He cursed the man who carried word of his birth to his father. He wished they had killed him the day he was born. He wished he had been born dead.

People who have moods like these come to talk with me. They think they are hopeless, and I might think so too if I did not have the example of men like Jeremiah to go by. In spite of his moods, Jeremiah rose to true greatness. So much so that many years later, when Christ asked His disciples, "Who do men say that I am?" they replied, "Some say you are Jeremiah."

Many felt that the highest tribute they could pay even Christ was to say that He was Jeremiah returned to earth. So I study Jeremiah to see what it was that made him great and caused him to overthrow those moods. I find four great strengths of his life.

(1) He was bound by a sense of duty. He did not always do the things he wanted to do, but rather did the things he felt he must do. We talk a great deal today about freedom, but we need also to talk a little about our obligations. Jeremiah's first step toward greatness was in doing what he ought to do, whether he liked it or not.

(2) He had a conviction that God's way was always the best way. It was not a question with him whether or not it was the popular way. Men might hiss him or applaud him, throw bouquets or bricks, he must take his stand on God's side.

(3) He had a great love in his heart. His people sometimes grieved and disgusted him, but still he loved them. He wanted to lead them right because he knew they were worth saving.

(4) Finally, he had the power of God with him. He said, "I feel within me as it were, a fire that burns my very being." You read in Jeremiah, "I am with thee, saith the Lord." And that assurance of God's presence and power was sufficient to overcome his weaknesses.

And today weak people like Jeremiah can rise to true greatness just as he did.

Pray About It

A GRADUATE OF one of the finest engineering schools in America came to see me. He has a brilliant scientific mind, but was somewhat mixed up in his personal life.

I suggested that we pray, but he assured me that he was not interested in prayer. He pointed out that being an engineer, he could never have any use for anything as unscientific as prayer.

I did not argue with him, but I gave him a little book and told him to talk to me again after he had read it. A few days later he said to me, "That is the greatest book I have ever read. Why, that book makes prayer scientifically respectable. I see the whole matter of religion in a different light now."

His reaction did not surprise me, because in the past year I have handed out about two hundred and fifty copies of that same little book, and the results it has produced are simply amazing.

The book is *Prayer, the Mightiest Force in the World,** by Dr. Frank C. Laubach. It contains only ninety-

* Fleming H. Revell Company.

five pages and is fascinatingly easy to read, but no person is ever the same after reading it.

Dr. Laubach was in Atlanta and came by to see me. He stayed an hour, but it seemed like five minutes. Before he left he prayed. I will never forget the first sentence of his prayer. He said, "Christ, I can see you standing here in this room and you are smiling."

In his book, Dr. Laubach explains that he is "personality zero" when he does not pray. But the moment he prays for people around him they respond with a "strange, sweet kindliness."

We Americans have spent a lot of money on books and courses on personality development. But if you really want a magnetic personality there is authentic scientific data showing that prayer is the way to get it.

At Old Farms, Connecticut, there is a school where scores of war-blinded veterans are learning "how to see without eyes."

The faculty these blind men use to "see" is called by many names, such as "sixth sense," "human radar," or "facial sight." Dr. Levine, of the school, says, "I cannot explain its mechanics, but I do know it works."

The two billion nerve and brain cells in the human body are miniature electric batteries. These minute batteries produce a magnetic field that projects our thoughts. Also, we possess "receiving sets" through which we receive the thoughts of others. This is one of the basic principles of prayer.

The newspapers tell us that America is building the hydrogen bomb, a bomb a thousand times more powerful than the atomic bomb. And we stand in awe at such power.

Yet right now at our disposal is the tremendous power of prayer, which is a far greater power than even the hydrogen bomb. Enough of us praying would bring peace on earth.

Prayer could bring a religious revival that would sweep the world. Prayer can transform a cold, lifeless church into a power house. Prayer can make radiant, happy, and victorious a person who before was worried, frustrated, and utterly defeated.

I could name no less than a hundred people whom I personally know who have been changed through prayer in the past few months.

But it bothers me when I realize that all around us there are so many people who are worried, nervous, tense, and actually sick. Yet, if they would pray, everything would be so different.

When I preach in my own church I know there are many people definitely praying for me. They tell me, but I can feel their prayers without them telling me. I know that prayer does have power.

If you have a problem—pray about it.

Just outside of Florence, Alabama, is a high bluff overlooking the Tennessee river. On top of the bluff is a lovely little park. I was in Florence for a revival, and one afternoon a friend took me out to that little park. It was wonderful to sit there watching that beautiful river. Just above us we could see one of those great hydro-electric dams built by T. V. A.

Presently I saw a tugboat coming up stream towing a

barge. It seemed to be huffing and puffing with all its might against the current. I asked my friend where the tug would stop. He told me it wouldn't stop. Instead, it would go up into the lake above. I wanted to see that, because I had never known of a tugboat that could fly and I did not know how else it could get over that big dam.

My friend explained that they had built a series of locks around the dam. I watched the tug tow the barge into the first lock, when its puffing ceased. The gates were closed below and opened above, and as the water came in, gradually the boat began to rise. Then it moved into the second lock and was lifted to a higher level. Finally, it had been lifted to the level of the lake and then, under its own power again, it could move on.

As I saw that, I, too, was lifted. I thought about how we huff and puff upstream against the swift currents of life. Sometimes we come to places where we cannot go on under our own power. Then I thought of a verse in Deuteronomy, "The eternal God is thy refuge, and underneath are the everlasting arms" (33:27). There is such a thing as resting back on the lifting power of God.

Dr. Fosdick once said, "He who cannot let go, cannot hang on; and he who loses serenity within, loses everything without." He points out that we must remember there are two aspects to every strong life; fruitage and rootage, activity and receptivity, tension and relaxation, working hard and resting back. God tells us through the Psalmist, "Be still, and know that I am God" (46:10). Sometimes we gain our greatest power by being still.

St. Augustine said, "Let my soul take refuge from the crowding turmoil of worldly thoughts beneath the shadow of Thy wings; let my heart, this sea of restless waves, find peace in Thee, O God."

I spoke along this line at a banquet in another city. Later I was sitting in the lobby of the hotel and the owner came over and sat down with me. He told me about a number of business interests he had. Then he told me about coming to his office one morning when he had so much to do and so many things to see about that he was in a state of confusion. He knew he could not possibly do all those things that day. He was worried and tense because of them.

Suddenly he got up from his desk, got his hat and told his secretary he would be out for the rest of the day and could not be reached. He went home, told his wife he did not want to be disturbed for any reason, and went to bed. He took his Bible and began reading the Psalms slowly and deliberately. He read until noon and then went downstairs for a light lunch. He went back and continued reading the rest of the afternoon.

He dressed for dinner and that night he enjoyed his meal as he had not enjoyed one in months. After dinner he stayed at home and entered into a quiet evening with his family. That night he slept wonderfully well, and when he went to his office the next morning he found that he could do all the things he needed to do and do them much better.

That man discovered for himself one of the most powerful forms of prayer—that of resting back upon the Divine Presence and being lifted by it. There is tremendous power in serene relaxation in God.

A very prominent business man said to me, "I used

to work on Sunday night, preparing my work for the coming week. But now I have discovered something. By going to church on Sunday night, participating in the song service, hearing a sermon and praying with a number of other people, I begin Monday morning much happier and better able to do a week's work."

If you feel the need of more power in your life, let me make a simple suggestion. Every morning for one week set aside ten minutes to carefully read the 23rd Psalm. Read it meditatively and prayerfully. At the end of that week you will see a distinct difference. Try it and see.

One of the most amazing statements I have ever read anywhere is this one: "Ask, and it shall be given you; seek, and ye shall find; knock, and it shall be opened unto you: for every one that asketh receiveth; and he that seeketh findeth; and to him that knocketh it shall be opened" (Matthew 7:7,8).

Those are the words of Christ, and He seems to be handing us a blank check on God and saying we can fill it in for anything we wish and it will be honored. Read the statement again, and you will see that He makes no restrictions, no limitations. And this promise is for "every one," He says.

It is really hard to believe, but those men who were closest to Christ certainly believed it. They saw Him work miracles and heard Him sway the multitudes with His sermons, but not one time did they ask Him to teach them those things. But they did say, "Lord, teach us to pray" (Luke 11:1).

They felt that if they learned to pray, then they had

the key to God's power. Jesus not only tells us of the unlimited power of prayer but gives us a simple formula that assures success in prayer every time it is used. There are three steps:

(1) Ask. To ask is to feel the need of something. Here we should be very definite. Before we pray, we should know exactly what we are praying for. We should take pencil and paper and carefully write it down. The reasons for our prayers should be clear and distinct before we actually begin praying.

Then, to ask is to be conscious of the fact that you are talking to a person because the very act of asking requires an answer. You can talk to a tree, but you cannot ask a tree something, because you know the tree cannot answer you.

To ask in prayer means that you must be conscious of the presence of God. Many times one is not conscious of God because there are other things between, such things as a dishonest act, a wrong attitude toward some other person, a questionable pleasure, a forsaken duty, a selfish spirit, etc.

Also, we need to prepare ourselves spiritually for our prayers. Preceding a prayer should be some exercise to help us to realize God's presence, such as the reading of a Psalm, quiet meditation, the singing of some familiar hymn.

This first step involves feeling the definite need and a consciousness of God's presence.

(2) Seek. Seeking is asking plus effort. God is not going to answer any prayer for you that you can answer for yourself. For me to pray, "Give us this day our daily

bread" means that I also am going to use all of my own energies and resources to provide the things I need.

I might want to pray for physical healing. Dr. William Sadler said, "Prayer is the greatest single power in the healing of disease." But prayer for healing means that I am going to observe the laws of health and use the means at my disposal. God is not going to do something for me that He knows my physician can do.

Jesus told us to pray for the kingdom of God on earth. But for me to pray for the wars to cease and the wrongs of earth to be eliminated means that I commit all of my *own* abilities and resources to bring that to pass.

(3) Knock. Knocking is asking plus effort plus persistence. Many times our prayers are delayed and we stop praying before the answer comes. Jesus told His first followers, "Tarry ye in the city of Jerusalem, until ye be endued with power from on high" (Luke 24:49). He told them what to pray for and to wait for the answer.

A minister friend of mine gave an invitation at the close of a service and a man came forward. The pastor whispered to the man, "Every day for twenty-seven years I have prayed for your soul." This minister had prayed the same prayer nearly ten thousand times before it was finally answered.

There is an encouraging word in Habakkuk 2:3, "Though it tarry, wait for it; because it will surely come."

Be definite as to your needs and sure of the presence of God, do all you can yourself, don't give up and Jesus said your prayers will be answered.

The 14th chapter of John is one of Jesus' last talks

with His disciples. He tells them they can do even greater things than He has done if they will believe (v. 12).

He had put before them a great vision. Now, He says, if you believe, that is, if you picture clearly in your mind the thing you want and put all your abilities into bringing it to pass, you can do marvelous things.

Then He assures them of the fact of the power of God which is available to help. He even says, "Whatsoever ye shall ask in my name, that will I do" (v. 13). That is a daring promise from one who has "never broken any promise spoken."

But we must remember that He said, "in my name." Prayer must conform to His spirit and be according to His will. And there are two main conditions we must keep in mind when we pray.

(1) God often refuses our immediate desires in order to be able to grant our larger needs. Let me illustrate: Our little girl said the other morning, "I don't want to go to school today. I want to stay home."

Had we granted her request we would have pleased her for the moment, but if we had continued to grant her request to stay at home, there would have come a day when she would condemn us severely for it. Though she doesn't realize it fully now, the larger desire of her heart is to get an education and prepare for a useful life.

When I was a boy there was a junk man in our town whom I liked very much. He had a horse and wagon and would go over the town buying scrap iron, old rags, and other junk. He would let me ride with him and drive the horse.

I had such a good time with him that I told my father

I wanted to be a junk man. It was really a deep desire of my heart.

Suppose my father had granted my request and had said, "All right. That is what you want, that is what you shall have. You shall be a junk man." For the moment I would have been very happy. But my father was wiser than I, and he was able to take the longer view of life for me.

He knew there were much greater opportunities ahead, and he kindly would turn down that immediate desire in order to make it possible to grant a much greater desire later on.

Tagore once said, "Thou didst save me by thy hard refusals." Isn't it wonderful that we have a Father who will carefully weigh every request of ours for our own good?

(2) A second important condition to remember is that God is not going to answer my prayer if it means hurting another one of His children.

One day I phoned for a reservation on an airplane for a date two days later. I was told that all reservations were taken. However, I asked them to take my phone number and call me if they had a cancellation.

I then said a prayer, asking God to help me get that reservation, and just two hours later they called me to say they had had a cancellation and I could have a seat. It seemed to me a direct answer to my prayer.

Another time I had a very different experience. I was in Charlotte, N. C., and wanted to fly back to Atlanta. I phoned and was told the plane was filled. Again I prayed about it and stood hopefully by, but the plane came and left without me.

God could have managed to put someone off that plane and make room for me. But the probability was that every person on that plane needed and wanted to go just as badly as I. And since all had applied before I did, it would not have been just or right for God to have hurt another one in order to favor me.

One of the greatest advantages of my life was growing up in a large family of children. We learned early that one should not ask for two pieces of pie if it meant another would not get any pie at all.

But you can pray with the full assurance that whatever you ask, if it is what you really need and if it is in harmony with God's plan for all of His children, then He will co-operate with you so that together with Him you can bring it to pass.

St. Paul said, "Pray without ceasing" (1 Thessalonians 5:17). One of the newer translations has that verse: "Let prayer be a habit," and that is a wonderful habit to develop.

My mother taught me my first prayer habit. Before I can remember I prayed every night this prayer: "Now I lay me down to sleep, I pray Thee, Lord, my soul to keep; if I should die before I wake, I pray Thee, Lord, my soul to take." Through the years I have prayed that same little prayer. I guess it would be possible for me to go to sleep without saying that prayer, but I have now become so addicted to it that I doubt that I will ever stop offering it.

A woman told me that when she was being rolled

into the operating room for an operation she was extremely frightened. That is a very difficult time in anyone's life. She wanted to pray but seemed not to be able to think of what to say. Then she thought of that little childhood prayer: "Now I lay me down to sleep . . ." and as she prayed, marvelous peace and calmness came into her mind and heart.

That little prayer is so easy to learn and, though it seems simple and childish, it is a marvelous thought to put into one's mind just before going to sleep. My wife has taught our children to add still another petition to it: "If I should live for other days, I pray Thee, Lord, to guide my ways."

Then I habitually pray when I sit down to eat a meal. That, too, is a habit that I developed before I can remember, because my father was always careful to have the blessing before we started eating. I used to think everybody had the blessing but I have discovered that this is a practice many homes have discarded.

I have suggested to husbands and wives who were not getting along so well to hold hands before each meal and say the blessing together. It may seem a little silly to some, but it will work wonders.

It has now become a habit with me to pray every time I see a funeral procession. Even though I do not know who it is, I know that in the cars behind that hearse are some saddened hearts who especially need help. It is not hard for me to pray, "Father, may just now that family especially feel the presence of thy sympathizing Jesus."

I always pray when I pass a church building. No matter what denomination it is, I know some people meet in that place to worship God and to gain inspiration for Christian service. Some people stand off and criticize the church but I know that my community is better because that church is there, so it comes naturally to me to pray for it.

When I see one in the uniform of our country, I am led to say a prayer. On some battlefield that boy or girl may lose his or her life defending me and all I hold dear. I think of the mother and father back home whose hearts are anxious. Maybe there are a young wife and some little children back home. Prayer for one in service comes very quickly with me. I especially pray that while he is away from home that boy may, above all things, hold his standards high.

Of course, I always pray for the sick. Sometimes I do not think it best to let the sick one know you are praying for him. But I always say a prayer. I pray that God may direct the mind and guide the hand of the physician. I ask a special blessing on the nurse who has such a difficult and important job. And I pray that the Great Physician may take a definite part in the case.

One of the great business leaders of our time is Mr. J. Arthur Rank. He has an elevator straight up to his office, but he does not use it. He prefers the stairs, and he calls them his "Prayer Stairs."

When he walks up in the morning he prays to God to guide him every step he takes that day. And he takes each step separately and deliberately as he prays. He finally arrives at the top in more ways than one.

In the morning he walks up, asking. In the evening

he walks down thanking God for the help He has given that day. Those stairs have become about the most important thing in Mr. Rank's life.

What are your prayer habits?

Faith Can Heal Our Emotional Sickness

MEDICAL SCIENCE IS making marvelous progress and I thank God for it. Just a few years ago, if a person had diabetes he died a horrible death. Today, however, a diabetic may live a normal, happy life. Diphtheria now has been conquered and one rarely ever hears of it.

Not long ago malaria was one of mankind's arch enemies, yet last year hardly 200 people in the United States died from it. The dread of pneumonia has about been removed. The defeat of tuberculosis is now in sight. There is new and wonderful hope for the cure of many forms of arthritis. Cancer is now fighting a losing battle. One after another of the dread diseases are being conquered by the onslaught of research and medicine.

In fact, it seems as though the physicians would work themselves out of a job. Yet, in spite of all our new discoveries, the doctors' offices and hospitals seem more crowded than ever before. And some of our doctors are saying that the cause of perhaps half our sickness is that we are not learning to meet life with calmness and faith.

One physician said, "It is the emotional man we are having difficulty in curing. Unfortunately, we have never been able to develop a scalpel with which we can go into the tangled ramifications of a man's mind and operate on that which is causing the mischief, namely, fear, anxiety, or guilt."

Then this physician said this: "There is only one physician who can heal and that is the Great Physician. And what a healer He is, what a genius in His touch as He lays His fingers, cool and strong, upon a man's mind!"

We do not need any new discoveries to heal the emotional man. In fact, you can turn to one of the oldest pieces of literature in existence and find the answer. Look at the 22nd chapter of Job. "Acquaint thyself with him," Job says, "and be at peace" (v. 21).

The fact is we are most acquainted with our problems. We give them first place in our thinking. We know them like a book. At any time we can recite our troubles, and even while we are asleep our minds are subconsciously thinking of them. Job says that is all wrong. Get acquainted with God if you want peace.

In that chapter are listed seven wonderful things that will happen to one who begins to think of God. "Good shall come unto thee." You can quit worrying about what tomorrow will bring forth, because, as Paul also points out, if you love God everything will eventually work out for good. If you know it will turn out good there is no need to worry.

"Thou shalt be built up." I think Eliphaz, who is talking to Job, means physically. Job had had a lot of troubles and he had worried himself sick. His troubles had led him to doubt God, but when his faith was straightened out, his health returned.

"Thou shalt lay up gold . . . and thou shalt have plenty of silver." Job had lost all his money, but when he put his life back in harmony with the laws of God he found that God was interested in his physical needs and would help him.

"Thou shalt have delight." Delight means "joyful satisfaction" and that is a wonderful state in which to live. "Thou shalt decree a thing, and it shall be established unto thee." You will not be defeated and frustrated in your endeavors.

"Light shall shine upon thy ways." Instead of stumbling along in the darkness of despair and groping in a haze of fear, you will be able to see where you are going and move forward with confidence.

"When men are cast down, then thou shalt say, There is lifting up." When periods of depression descend on you, your spirit will be lifted and your heart set to singing again. Read Job 22:21-30. It seems almost too good to be true, yet down through the centuries, those who have tried it have found it to be true.

Dale Carnegie has tried it. He says, "When I am so busy that I do not have time to pray then I know it is time to pray. I just forget everything and go to church. I yield myself to God, and the tension and anxiety go out of me and peace and power come in."

Notice, finally, that Eliphaz says to Job, "He shall save the humble person." God can never come into your life until you really feel the need of Him. It is better to kneel before Him as an expression of our humility. That is why I invite people in my own church to kneel at the altar.

"Acquaint now thyself with him, and be at peace."

A woman from another city came to see me. She was so afraid she was actually trembling and she sat on the edge of the chair as though she thought it might fall any minute.

Finally she told me her story. She is a singer. She has one of the best teachers in the country and her teacher says she really has a great talent. She wants to sing in opera and her teacher feels she is about ready. She has worked years to get to that place.

But she told me that every time she is ready to sing before an audience a paralyzing fear grips her and she goes all to pieces. In the city where she lives they were soon to give an opera, and she had the leading rôle, but she was worried sick over it. She could not sleep at night.

I talked to her about God. How that God had given her a wonderful voice and that He not only expected her to use it, but that also He would help her use it. I taught her a few simple ways to practice God's presence and we had a prayer together.

Later she wrote me as follows:

> The strength and courage that I gained through faith in God made possible my giving a brilliant performance. I sang as I have never sung before. Everyone was amazed, but no one more than I.
>
> The feeling of a job well done, that I thought would never be mine, has come so quickly that it is indeed a miracle and I am truly humble.
>
> As I stood off stage and heard my cue, my heart began to pound but I immediately said to myself, "Easy does it." [I had taught her how to say that.] As I walked on stage I prayed, "He leadeth me beside the still waters." [I had told her to

form mental pictures of still waters as she said that.] I was filled with a feeling of confidence and jubilance.

That is not an isolated example. I have seen the simple principles of faith change the lives of many people. As I write this I have a letter before me from a woman in Atlanta.

She was so worried she could not go to work. She has a slight physical handicap that had begun to get the best of her. And then her boss would say harsh and cutting things to her. I had talked to her about praying for this boss instead of fearing her. I told her how to picture herself mentally as succeeding. We talked about the power of faith.

Now she writes:

> My boss called me in for a conference, said complimentary things about my work, and gave me a raise in salary. She has made me the highest paid person in her department, and was kind in every word she said.
>
> I am so thankful that I have learned to pray and to believe in myself again.

These principles of faith are found throughout the Bible. St. Paul had a handicap that could have wrecked his life. He prayed about it and God answered by saying: "My grace is sufficient for thee" (II Corinthians 12:9). That is, God was promising Paul the strength to overcome whatever handicap or condition he was facing.

As a result, Paul later triumphantly declared, "We are more than conquerors through him that loved us" (Romans 8:37).

This is the faith that built America and made it great. Read "The Star-Spangled Banner," our national anthem.

Francis Scott Key had gone out to the British fleet under a flag of truce. He was detained on board the British ship while the bombardment of Fort Henry took place.

It was a terrible night for the young patriot. The struggling colonies of America were against the vast resources of the great British empire. All night long the heavy guns had pounded Fort Henry.

But in the morning he saw "by the dawn's early light the star-spangled banner yet waving," and was inspired to write his famous song. The climax of that song is found in the last verse: "Then conquer we must, when our cause it is just. And this be our motto: 'In God is our trust.' "

When you put your faith in God and do your best, things usually do work out all right.

Jesus said, "If ye have faith as a grain of mustard seed, ye shall say unto this mountain, Remove hence to yonder place; and it shall remove, and nothing shall be impossible unto you" (Matthew 17:20).

Many of us misread that verse. We think of a grain of mustard seed as a little thing and conclude that Jesus was saying, If ye have only a little faith. A grain of sand is also little, but Jesus did not say as a grain of sand. The difference is that a grain of sand is a dead, fixed thing, while a grain of mustard seed is a live thing with capacity for growth and development.

What Jesus was saying is that if we will take what faith we have, even though it seems small and insignificant, and begin to use it, we will accomplish things that before seemed impossible.

It does not mean that suddenly you will accomplish everything overnight. The mustard seed does not grow that way. Instead, the seed is planted in the ground. As it grows it draws food and warmth from the earth. Even though it is buried in the ground, it realizes there is sunshine above and it begins to push up.

The mustard seed is not discouraged because it is little. Instead, it pictures itself as a large plant, and it is never satisfied until it reaches its fullest possible maturity.

And Jesus is telling you that, instead of worrying about how little you have or how meager your opportunities are, if you will take what you have and begin to use it, drawing on every possible resource as you go, never quitting, you will grow bigger than the mountain of any problem in your life.

I thought of this verse one day when I took my three children out to climb Stone Mountain. For Charles, Jr., who is a big, husky boy weighing 170 pounds, the mountain was no obstacle at all. He could walk to the top of it and down the other side about as easily as he could walk on level ground.

But for Franklin and Mary Jane, ages six and seven, it was a great obstacle in their way. Their little legs would get tired and we had to stop for rest now and then. But one day they will be large and strong enough so that the obstacle of the mountain will have been removed for them. The mountain will still be there, but they will be able to walk over it without difficulty.

So in life. There are mountains of difficulties in our way. In some instances it is possible to remove the difficulties. In other instances it is possible for us to grow to the point where we can overcome the difficulty.

Instead of growing, some people become dominating

and abusive. They are the ones who complain the loudest, who are the most prejudiced, and who are the hardest to get along with. They blow themselves up like a toy balloon and become self-centered snobs.

Recently I was conducting a series of revival services in another city. More people attended the services than could be seated in the main sanctuary of the church, so some loud speakers were put in the basement and the overflow crowd was asked to sit down there. Some refused to go and went back home. Others went, but complained about it.

But after the service one night I noticed a man sitting, quietly waiting to speak to me. When I met him he told me his name. I nearly fell over, because he is one of the greatest judges the South has ever produced. He is a famous and beloved man.

He told me that he had not arrived in time to get a seat. The ushers wanted to have someone get up and give him his seat. But the judge would not hear of it. Graciously he went down to the basement and heard the service over the speakers. He had grown to the point where having to take a second place was no obstacle to him.

If you would develop growing faith you must first have a purpose, and that purpose must stand before you clear and inviting. Then you must consider the possibilities of action and decide on what action seems best. Then you must get started toward achieving that purpose.

Then your faith goes to work. Instead of concentrating on the difficulties in your path, you concentrate on your own abilities and strengths. You begin using all you have, keeping in mind that "the things which are impossible with men are possible with God" (Luke 18:27), and the mountains that have been blocking your way will be removed.

A physician made a study of the matters his patients were afraid of. Forty per cent of the fears were over things that never happened. Thirty per cent were over past events which were beyond control. Twelve per cent were fearful of their health, though their illnesses were imaginary. Ten per cent were afraid over the well-being of some loved one.

Only eight per cent of the fears of this physician's patients had any real cause which needed attention. Ninety-two per cent of their fears were needless. My own observations would certainly agree with that analysis of the fears of people.

Fear is only a thought in the mind. It may be a thought that has been driven so deeply and has become so firmly fixed in one's mind that it has become an obsession, but it is still just a thought. And the only way to get a thought out of your mind is to substitute a stronger thought.

I know only one pattern of thought stronger than the fear pattern and that is faith. Just as penicillin kills germs in your body, so faith kills fear in your mind. I often wish I had faith in capsule form and could prescribe three or four capsules a day to those who need them. However, there are several ways one can take doses of faith.

(1) One way is to read your Bible regularly every day. When you read something it sets up a mysterious process. The word becomes an image on the retina of your eye.

Then that image is transferred to your mind and becomes a thought. It is a process of digestion. The Bible is a book filled with God, with whom nothing is hopeless or impossible. Faith results naturally.

I have before me a letter from a high-school girl. She wrote me a month ago that because of a prolonged illness she had to stay out of school for two years. When she went back she was older and larger than the others, which made her so self-conscious that she was miserable and afraid.

I wrote suggesting that she completely saturate her mind with the Twenty-third Psalm, that she memorize it completely and repeat it immediately on waking in the morning. She was to repeat it to herself at least six times a day for a month.

Now she writes in part:

> I did what you told me and now I have been elected president of my Sunday-school class, have been accepted a member in the Tri-Hi-Y Club, and I believe everyone sees the difference in me. I don't think I have ever been as happy as I am now and I know I will never be afraid again.

Some time ago I suggested that if one would read carefully the Gospel of Matthew ten times it would change his life. I have scores of letters from people in the South who have written me of wonderful things that have happened to them because they did that.

(2) You get faith by going regularly to church. Nothing is more catching than the spirit of a large crowd of people. Frequently I have been so inspired by a congregation that I said things in my sermon I had never thought of before. And usually those are the best things I say.

Especially is that true in the Sunday night service, when the atmosphere is so warm and free.

You see, the music, the songs, and the words of the minister fall on our eardrums. Those sounds are transferred to the brain to become thoughts and ideas. If you hear words of faith they create patterns of faith in your mind that drive out the fears lurking there.

(3) A third way to gain faith is to consecrate your life to something greater than yourself. Maxwell Anderson wrote a play entitled, "Candle In The Wind." It tells the story of a young American girl struggling against the ruthless Nazi rulers of occupied Paris. She is struggling to liberate her lover.

She is only a young girl. Just a candle in the wind, but she is sustained and strengthened by the feeling that she is on the side of justice and right, and that her own great nation of America is behind her.

And when one feels his cause is just and right and that he has the blessing of God, he experiences a surge of strength and confidence that overcomes all fear.

Why We Worry and How to Stop

Rabbi Liebman's elder friend was certainly right when he told him that the most important possession of all is "peace of mind." Even if one has health, love, beauty, talent, power, riches and fame—the essentials that the rabbi listed as a young man—still, if one lacks peace of mind life is a hideous torment and an intolerable burden.

There are four main reasons why so many people do not have this blessed inner peace.

(1) We worry about the things we do not have and so become dissatisfied with the things we have. Once I was the pastor of a little church far back in the mountains. In the community there was an old man with whom I spent a lot of time and from whom I learned a lot. He was a wise philosopher.

He would tell me of life as it used to be. How very little the people had, but yet how happy they were. But one day the mail man left a mail-order catalogue at a neighbor's house. The people began to look at it, first wonderingly and then longingly.

Soon every home in the community had one of the catalogues. The old man would shake his head sadly as he told how the people forgot the beauty of the mountains around them and turned away from the things that used to mean so much when they turned the pages of the catalogue and thought of the many things they did not possess.

I can bring my children any little toy and they will be happy with it. But if I let them go into the store with me to buy one, then, no matter what we buy, they will be unhappy because they forget about the one we buy in thinking of all the toys we did not buy.

On his eightieth birthday, someone asked Bishop Herbert Welch the secret of his serene spirit. He replied, "As I grow older, life becomes simpler because I see the essentials more clearly in the evening light."

(2) We develop a "crisis psychology." Some crisis is always coming along, such as a debt or a sickness or the war or one of a thousand other things, and, before we realize it, life has become a constant crisis.

I read somewhere of a dinner table trick the great singer Enrico Caruso used frequently. He would hold a slender glass high in the air and sing an ascending scale until he came to a high note which he would repeat until the constant vibration shattered the glass.

And one crisis after another in a life will shatter it. Robert Greenleaf Whittier prayed, "Take from our souls the strain and stress, and let our ordered lives confess the beauty of thy peace." We must learn not to make a crisis out of every unhappy experience that comes along.

(3) Our inner conflicts destroy our inner peace. Man is made with both a higher and a lower nature, and there is a constant struggle between the two. Jesus had perfect inner peace because He was perfectly good.

I suppose that if a person were completely bad he would have a measure of peace. And sometimes we think we can get rid of our inner conflicts by letting down and living on the lower animal level.

The prodigal son tried that, but eventually his longing for home destroyed all possibility of happiness in a hog pen. As a young man, St. Augustine tried to find peace in every form of sensual indulgence. Eventually he had to come back to God, saying, "Our souls are restless until they find their rest in Thee."

(4) There are conflicts between ourselves and other people that destroy our peace. Our feelings are hurt. We carry a grudge. We have an unforgiving spirit.

Someone has suggested that instead of praying "Forgive us our trespasses, as we forgive those that trespass against us," we pray, "Forgive me my trespasses as I forgive John Doe for what he has done to me." There is marvelous power in a personal prayer like that.

"And the peace of God, which passeth all understanding, shall keep your hearts and minds through Christ Jesus" (Philippians 4:7).

The word "worry" does not occur in the Bible, but often occurs in the minds of many people. Worry robs a life of its power and joy, makes many people sick, and even can destroy the desire to live. Sometimes we can conquer a thing if we know its cause, so I would like to list some of the causes of worry.

(1) We worry because we are hurt. Sometimes we are hurt because of the loss of something. We lose our material possessions, or our health, friends, job, or one of

a number of things. Even more often we worry because we fear that we may lose something.

Life hurts many because of what it withholds. We dream, plan, and struggle, but the best prizes elude us. Hope is a wonderful thing but continued unrealized hope has the power to break a heart.

Many are hurt because of what happens to someone else. One whom we love is hurt, but, more often, we worry because of the success of someone else. Envy and jealousy have the power to hurt terribly.

(2) Another reason we worry is because we refuse to accept life as it is. I am not a fatalist, but there are some things in life that we cannot change and to refuse to accept them is a major cause of worry.

Someone wrote these lines about the weather: "After all, man is nothing but a fool; when it's hot he wants it cool; when it's cool he wants it hot; he always wants it the way it's not." There are many things that we cannot change and that we must accept as graciously as we can. Certainly it does no good to worry about them.

(3) Many worry because they refuse to accept their own limitations. I have heard people say, "I can do anything anybody else can do." That is a foolish and silly statement.

God did not put all His stars in any one person's sky or plant all His flowers in any one garden. One may feel that God planted only common daisies in his yard and worry about the lovely roses growing in his neighbor's garden. We will not make the daisies of our own lives any prettier by being jealous of the roses in our neighbors' lives.

At a banquet I sat by a very wealthy man. This man has accumulated several millions of dollars. He told me about some of his business interests and I found myself a bit envious. I was the speaker for the banquet, and after I finished my speech and sat down, my wealthy friend said to me, "I would give a million dollars if I could make a speech like that."

You cannot do everything others can do, but you can do some things well and that is what counts for most in your life.

(4) Many times we worry because we are too self-centered. Arnold Bennett said: "The best cure for worry is to go deliberately forth and try to lift the gloom off somebody else."

In the Sermon on the Mount Jesus tells us not to be too concerned with what we are going to eat and wear and all the daily things of life. Instead, He says, lose your life in some great enterprise, make your life count for something, and you will get along all right (Matthew 6:25-34).

Once a soldier said to his buddy, "You are wounded." The other soldier replied, "Well, I declare, I had not noticed it." That soldier had been in a battle and had been lifted out of himself.

(5) Another reason people worry is because they are at war with their own conscience. We face decisions we dare not make, hear calls to duty we will not answer, commit acts that violate our own ideals.

The prophet of old pleaded with the people, "Choose you this day whom ye will serve" (Joshua 24:15). Once there was a king named Redwall. He built two altars of worship, one for God and the other for the devil.

In explaining to a friend, he said, "God has wonderful power and so has the devil, so the best thing to do is try to keep on the good side of both of them." Some try that today, but Jesus said, "No man can serve two masters" (Matthew 6:24).

(6) A main cause of worry is lack of faith. Faith and worry just cannot live in the same mind. Faith in yourself and faith in God bring peace and power.

One of the most common fears of people is the fear that something bad is going to happen tomorrow or some time in the future. An extreme example is a man who told me he was afraid he might die any day. I asked why he thought about dying, and he said he was afraid that he had heart trouble.

I suggested to him to see a physician. He had been examined and the doctor had told him his heart was in good condition, but he was still afraid. I asked why he was afraid of dying and he said he might go to hell. I suggested that he repent of his sins and get ready to die. He claimed he had done that, but still was afraid.

He told me that he worried because his wife might leave him. I asked if she had ever indicated in any way that she was thinking of leaving. He said no, but that he had known of other men's wives leaving them and he thought that his wife might leave him, too.

Then, he was afraid that he might lose his job. I asked if he was doing his work all right and if his employer had ever said anything about firing him. He told me he was doing a good job and his boss has always seemed pleased with his work. Still, other men have been fired and he might be, too.

This is such an extreme example that it seems almost incredible. Yet there are many people suffering with a fear of something dreadful happening. We allow the thought of some possible disaster to rob our lives of all the joy and beauty that are ours.

The ability to think of the future is one of the greatest blessings God has given to man. If wisely used, this ability will cause us to plan and work for tomorrow. The realization that there will be a tomorrow is the basis of all hope. Man is the only creature on earth that can hope, because only men have the ability to think in terms of a tomorrow. But this marvelous gift of God can become perverted, and then it breeds misery and fear.

In the last letter he wrote, St. Paul said to a young man named Timothy, "Stir up the gift of God which is in thee." That is, stand up and become a real man by using all the strength and abilities that you possess. "For," the great Apostle said, "God hath not given us the spirit of fear; but of power, and of love, and of a sound mind" (II Timothy 1:6,7).

That is, when you do your best and have faith in God, Paul is saying you have powers and abilities you did not know about before. You have a love for people instead of a fear of people. And your mind is clear, so that you can work out your problems and decide the best courses of action.

A letter from someone who had heard me on the radio took me to task for not preaching the gospel. Instead of telling so many stories about people I meet, I should read the four Gospels and tell what Jesus said. But that person absolutely fails to understand the principles of Jesus. He enunciated great principles and then He looked for the illustrations of those principles in everyday life about Him.

That is what I try to do. I study the principles of Christ and then I watch to see them working in the lives of people. That is the reason I believe so completely in the power of Christian faith. I see it working wonders in the lives of people. Here are two examples:

I stopped to get a shoe shine. The Negro man recognized me and said that he had heard me say over the radio that faith in God would change your life. He told me he knew I was telling the truth because he had tried it. I asked for his story and I want to quote his exact words:

> One time I got fired off my job. I looked for work but couldn't find nothing right off. My wife and chillun were hungry and we didn't have nobody to turn to. One night I told my wife we could look to the good Lord. So we got on our knees. The next day I went out looking for work, took the first job I found and we have had plenty ever since. The Lord shore will take care of you if you trust Him.

I might have pointed out to him that he helped the Lord by going out and doing what he could. But the point is, he is a happy man.

Henry Ford would often go and sit before a big clock he had put up in Greenwich Village. When the clock struck the hour the following little song would be sung: "Lord, through this hour be Thou our guide, that through Thy power no foot may slide."

Then Mr. Ford would say this little prayer: "Lord,

you are with me through the next hour, and whatever problem I have to face, I will not be afraid." Mr. Ford carried heavy responsibilities, but he lived a long and serene life.

Jesus gives us two ways to keep from worrying about tomorrow. (1) One way is to live a day at a time. He says, "Take therefore no thought for the morrow: for the morrow shall take thought for the things of itself. Sufficient unto the day is the evil thereof" (Matthew 6:34).

Moffatt translates that verse to read: "So do not be troubled about tomorrow; tomorrow will take care of itself. The day's own trouble is quite enough for the day."

Robert Quillen told of a famous old naturalist who began to cut trees to build a log house. A friend said, "Isn't that a big undertaking for a man of your years?" The old naturalist replied, "It would be if I thought of chopping the trees, sawing the logs, skinning the bark, laying the foundation, erecting the walls and putting on the roof. Carrying the load all at once would exhaust me. But it isn't so hard to cut down this one tree and that is all I have to do today."

Sir William Osler, the famous physician and professor of medicine at Johns Hopkins University, tells of one night when he was worried sick. His final examination was coming up the next day, and he was anxious not only about that but also about his future.

That night he picked up a copy of Carlyle's works and happened to read this familiar sentence: "Our main business is not to see what lies dimly at a distance, but to do what lies clearly at hand."

Years later, when he returned to his native England

to be knighted by the king, he said, "More than anything else I owe whatever success I have had to the power of settling down to the day's work and doing it to the best of my ability, letting the future take care of itself."

Isn't it true that most of our worries are borrowed from some other day? We worry about mountains we will never have to climb, about streams we will never have to cross, about situations we will never have to meet.

I refer often to the women going to the tomb of Jesus that first Easter morning. It must have been a glorious time, with the sun just rising in majestic splendor, the crisp, cool early spring air, and the lovely wild flowers growing along the way. But they missed all that. Instead, they were worrying about who would roll the stone away. Yet, when they got there, they found the stone had already been rolled away. All their worry was about a situation which had been taken care of before they reached it.

We must remember also that living a day at a time refers just as much to yesterday as it does to tomorrow. God is far more ready to forgive us than we are to forgive ourselves. Suppose you did make a mistake yesterday, do you expect to keep the shadow hanging over you for the rest of your life? If you can correct the wrong, then do so and go ahead about the business of living today.

(2) There is a second reason why Jesus said, "Take therefore no thought for the morrow." The word "therefore" is it. By that he meant that we are not orphans in this world. He gave two illustrations: One was the birds of the air. The other was the lilies of the field.

Jesus asks each of us if we are not more important

than a bird or a flower that will soon die, never to live again. And if God cares for the birds, even noting the fall of each one, and if He so beautifully clothes the lilies, then how much more, Jesus says, will God do for one of His own children, made in His own image? (Matthew 6:26-30).

So the two cures for worrying about tomorrow are, first, put your best into living this one day, and, second, put your trust in the God who made both you and this world, realizing that step by step He will carry you through.

Three sentences from St. Paul express this faith: "If God be for us, who can be against us?" "My God shall supply all your needs." "All things work together for good to them that love God."

Security Can Be Yours

ONE OF THE greatest desires of the human heart is to feel secure. Some psychologists even say that our desire for security is an instinct. Certainly we all want security, and many of us do not have it.

Jesus preached to people about this feeling of security. In the sixth chapter of Matthew He tells us to recognize the fact that God knows and loves us and is able to provide.

He points out the birds of the air and the fact that they get along all right. He tells them to notice the lilies of the field and how beautifully God clothes them. Wherefore, Jesus says, if God so clothe the grass of the field, which will live but a day, will He not do so much more for you, who will live eternally?

Certainly God wants us to feel secure, and, above and beyond all other things, a feeling of God's presence brings security. Never a week passes that someone does not tell or write me that praying at the altar has given him a new inner security and peace.

And I would like to list some other steps that will help bring security:

(1) Train yourself to be happy with what you can afford. I know well some very miserable people who are trying to maintain a standard of living beyond their means. It is a terrible way to live.

(2) No matter how little you earn, save a little. I do not sell life insurance, but I could because I believe in it strongly. A few dollars invested or put in a savings account will bring far more satisfaction than some gadget we strain to buy.

(3) Never lose the spirit of adventure. Be willing to dream and to dare. Columbus would never have discovered a new world had he always been afraid to get out of sight of land. In life there is something greater than merely taking care of one's self. Be willing to risk a little.

(4) Get acquainted with as many people as you can. There is strong security in your friendships. Also, when you come to know the problems of other people and see how they have overcome them, you will gain more confidence.

(5) Realize that there is always a way out if you will do your best. Even your troubles may prove your greatest blessings.

I had an experience recently that illustrates the last point. I was driving down to Augusta to speak to the Georgia Druggists Convention. I left early enough to get there but had no time to waste. Just as I reached Loganssville my car broke down. The garage man told me he could fix it, but that it would not be ready before afternoon. My speech in Augusta was to be at noon.

I tried to rent a car but could find none. It was two hours until the next bus and that was too late for me. So

I did the only thing left, I stood on the highway and started hitch-hiking. In a few minutes a man in a nice car came along and picked me up. He was going to Athens.

In Athens I stopped at the Buick place to see my friend, Mr. Warren Thurmond, about borrowing a car. He had a new demonstrator he would be glad for me to drive to Augusta, if I didn't mind. I didn't mind. While I was talking with Mr. Thurmond, I noticed a beautiful new supersedan in his display room.

I wistfully thought out loud how I would like to have a car like that. He said he would sell it to me, but I assured him it was beyond my financial reach. He said he would help me to buy it. I had been preaching in a revival the week before in his church in Athens, and he felt the revival had done good. So he made me the finest proposition anybody has ever given me. I could not turn him down.

When I came back that afternoon, he had the new car ready, and sent up to Logansville for my old one. So it turned out that my car breaking down was not a tragedy but one of the finest blessings I have had. Because of the break-down, I made my trip in a better car than I had, and ended up by owning a beautiful brand new one that otherwise I never would have bought.

There is always a way out if you do not give up.

What is the most happiness-producing lesson one can learn in life? I would hesitate to answer that question, because there are many things one can learn that will make for a happy life. However, along with some others, I would list a lesson that St. Paul learned. He said: "I have learned, in whatsoever state I am, therewith to be content" (Philippians 4:11).

The man who learned to be content had no home, no wife, and no children. He had a few close friends, just before he died he saw most of them desert him and turn away. He was brutally beaten many times. He spent many nights in jail. Most of his life was lived in poverty, and often he was denied the barest necessities. He knew what it was to be hungry and cold.

But, in spite of all his hardships, he was a radiant, happy man who never complained. He learned to be content. The word contentment comes from two Latin words meaning "to hold together." We sometimes hear one say, "I went to pieces." Contentment means that one is held together.

Of course, there is a sense in which one should not be contented. We should never be contented with all the wrongs and injustices of the world. There is such a thing as a divine discontent that drives one ever upward and onward. St. Paul himself says, "I count not myself to have apprehended: . . . I press toward the mark" (Philippians 3:13, 14). Contentment does not necessarily mean that you are satisfied, neither does it mean weak resignation. It does mean that you have an inner peace and power that holds you together and enables you to be and do your best.

Notice that the wise Apostle says, "I have learned to be content." It wasn't something that happened to him in a quick, miraculous manner. He did not have a snappy little formula. It was something he worked at and gradually learned.

Every Sunday my soul is stirred as I listen to Dr. John Cottle play our big organ. Sometimes during the week, when there is no one at the church but me, I turn on the organ and with two fingers pick out a simple tune. I find myself wishing that I could play like Dr. Cottle.

But the reason I cannot play is simply because I have not learned how. Dr. Cottle wanted to learn to play and he worked at it. Hour upon hour has he studied and practiced. There is no quick, easy way to learn, but most of us can learn whatever we want to.

Conradi put a sparrow egg in the nest of a canary. The mother canary hatched the egg and mothered the little sparrow from the day of its birth. Day by day the little sparrow heard the singing of the canary, and by the time it was grown it could sing like a canary. Conradi said it was very difficult to tell the difference between the singing of the sparrow and the singing of the canary.

If a common sparrow can learn to sing like a canary, then it is reasonable to believe that any of us can learn almost anything into which we put our mind and effort. We can learn always to have inside a calm, cooling contentment, no matter what the conditions may be outside.

Here is a simple way to start learning. Try it for just one week, and you will feel a distinct difference. When you awaken in the morning, and before you get out of bed, tell yourself that it is going to be a great day to live.

As you sit down to breakfast look at your wife and tell yourself and her that you have the most wonderful wife in the world. When you go to your office or your work, instead of complaining about the crowded bus or the heavy traffic, think how wonderful it is that so many other people have a job and are going to work.

This may sound a bit silly, but keep it up all day. Look for something good in every situation and concentrate on that. Keep that up just one week and the next week-end will be one of the happiest you have ever spent.

One other thing: Paul never learned to be content until the day he said, "What shall I do, Lord?" (Acts 22:10). He never learned contentment until he learned first consecration. A long time ago Job said, "Acquaint now thyself with him, and be at peace; thereby good shall come unto thee" (Job 22:21).

When one feels that his life is in harmony with the will of God, then, no matter what his lot in life may be, he has joy in living it.

"Be of good cheer, my brother, for I feel the bottom and it is sound." Those are the words of Hopeful in *Pilgrim's Progress.* You remember how, in their journey to the City of God, they came to the last dark river. Hopeful, as hope always does, lead the way and, in the very midst of the river, called back that assuring word.

We now have come to the end of a year. As we look back over the journey we see many trials and hardships, but for many there is still a dark river ahead. Now, there are two ways of looking at the future. One way is to concentrate on the dark river, the other way is to say with Hopeful, "Be of good cheer, my brother, for I feel the bottom and it is sound." That is, think of the sound bottom instead of the river.

A man who was thinking of taking his life came to see me. He told me he had lost everything and therefore had no reason to live. I asked what he had lost, and he said it was his business and every dollar he had. I used a technique with him that I learned from Dr. Norman Vincent Peale.

I took a sheet of paper and drew a line down the center. On one side I wrote "losses" and on the other side wrote "assets." Under "losses" I wrote "business and money." I asked if he had lost anything else. He said, "That is all, but that is everything."

"Has your wife left you?" I asked. "Oh, no," he said, "she still loves me and she has a job in a department store to help us out." So under assets I wrote "wife." I asked about his children. He has two, and he assured me they were still loyal to him. So I listed "children" as an asset.

Then I asked him if he had forgotten all that he had learned in his twenty-five years of business. Of course, he had not, and he talked about how much more he knew now than he knew when he started. So I listed "knowledge and experience" as an asset.

"Is there as much opportunity in America today as there was twenty-five years ago?" was my next question. He assured me there was much more opportunity today. So we put down "opportunity." His health is good, so we listed that. Finally I asked if he believed in God. He did, so we wrote down God.

Then I told him about Hopeful in *Pilgrim's Progress,* and pointed out how he, too, had come to a dark river. It isn't easy to lose a business you have worked twenty-five years to build. But, instead of concentrating on his losses, we talked about concentrating on his assets. After all, a man with a loyal wife, children, experience, opportunity, health, and God should be able to say sincerely, "Be of good cheer, my brother, the bottom is sound."

He left me, realizing that he did have a firm foundation on which to start building again. I believe he went out with "good cheer" in his heart.

Just as a business takes inventory at the end of the year, so should we. All of us have lost things this year. Some have buried loved ones. There have been very few weeks this year in which I have not stood with from one to three families and buried one dear to their hearts. That is a loss one never quite overcomes.

Some have lost material things. Some have lost opportunities. Some have lost ideals, or faith, or many other things. And in the midst of a severe loss one's mind plays a very harsh trick on him. Filled with thoughts of that loss, one easily believes he has lost everything. So when we take inventory let us not forget to list on the other side of the page our "assets," the things we have not lost.

This is what is called positive thinking. One of the most powerful forms of prayer is the prayer of "affirmation." This type of prayer does not beg God to give something or to do something. Rather does it remember and affirm certain facts. For example, "The Lord is my shepherd; I shall not want." That is a statement of fact and also a very powerful prayer. "Our father which art in heaven" is a petition of affirmation.

I frequently say to people who have doubts and fears, tell me some things you are sure of, tell me what you believe. When you begin to concentrate on the positive side through faith, the mountains of your losses, disappointments, doubts and fears are removed, and nothing is impossible unto you (Matthew 17:20).

Into a pastor's study on a main thoroughfare of a great city come people with all kinds of needs. Many need spiritual help, and many need physical help, too. There come men without jobs, whose families are hungry. There are those without any money, with the rent long past due. There are young people trying to get started in a life's work.

And often these people say they do not want any of that "prayer and faith" stuff. They want something practical. I spend a lot of time trying to help people who have material needs. And one of my favorite stories is found in the Twenty-first chapter of John.

Seven of the disciples had gone fishing. Christ had been crucified, and Judas, their treasurer, had committed suicide. These men did not go fishing for the sport of it, they went because they were broke and hungry. They fished all night and caught nothing.

In the gray dawn of the morning they saw a man standing on the shore. It was Jesus but they did not immediately recognize Him. Note carefully His first word to them. He did not condemn them for any wrong they had done. He did not scold because they had not done what they should have done. Instead, He said, "Have ye any meat?"

He was concerned about their physical welfare. Then He used His power to help them. He told them to cast on the other side, and they did, and caught 153 large fish. It was probably the biggest catch any of them had ever seen.

Here is the supreme proof to me that Jesus understands the needs of people—the fact that when they reached shore He had a fire going and breakfast cooked, and said the most welcome words any fisherman ever heard who had been out all night: "Come and dine." Or, "Breakfast is ready."

The last time I went fishing at night I had the same success these disciples had had. I "caught nothing," and that morning all we had for breakfast was fat back, syrup, and hush-puppies. But I was so hungry that the food tasted like a T-bone steak, strawberry jam, and angel-food cake.

Jesus had risen just a few days before. That morning He might have revealed Himself by duplicating the splendor of the transfiguration. Or He might have had a choir come down from heaven and sing as the heavenly choir had sung at His birth. Or He might have had legions of angels to demonstrate His power.

But see what He did. Though His feet were bruised, He walked over the rocky beach and gathered firewood. Then, though His hands had been nail-pierced, He cleaned fish and cooked breakfast for seven hungry men.

This story teaches us that faith in Him leads one to be both spiritual and practical. We need to remember that the same Christ who taught us to pray, "Forgive us our sins," also taught us to pray, "Give us this day our daily bread." That the same God who gave Moses the Ten Commandments also rained down bread from heaven when the people were hungry.

I am not forgetting that Jesus said: "Take no thought for your life, what ye shall eat, or what ye shall drink;

nor yet for your body, what ye shall put on" (Matthew 6:25).

But I also remember that the reason He said that was not because what we eat and wear is unimportant, but rather to tell us we need not worry about these things. He pointed out that God feeds the birds and clothes the lilies and that He will do far more for His children.

A few months ago a man who had just lost his job came to my study. He was worried and afraid, and did not know which way to turn. I knew of no jobs open that he might be suited for, so I suggested that we pray about it. On our knees, I asked God to please help him, and I felt an immediate answer.

I told the man that I felt confident that he had nothing to worry about, that if he would do his best to find another job, the right thing would come very quickly. I can report that the very next day he did find a better job than he had lost, that he is at church every Sunday, and is today one of the happiest men I know.

It is not a sin to make money. It is not wrong to desire some of the material comforts of life. And I am thankful I have a God who is mindful of my material needs and is ever ready to help me.

Never forget that The Risen Lord with His own nail-pierced hands cooked breakfast for seven hungry fishermen.

A letter from a young woman thirty-one years old tells me that for her "life is not worth living," and that she is going to end it. I wrote her as best I could, but a few days later she did take her own life.

If not to that extreme, there are many people who

feel life is not worth much to them. Instead of greeting each new day with thrilling joy, they would rather skip it entirely. And some would rather skip all of their remaining days.

A recent trip brought to my mind the difference in the joys people might experience as they travel along through life. My wife and I drove up to Trion, Georgia, where I was to speak at a banquet for women given by the Rotary Club.

It was a lovely afternoon, and we left an hour earlier than necessary, drove slowly, and enjoyed the scenery. The trees were lovely in their new spring dresses, and the mountains in the distance reminded me of the verse in Psalm 121, "I will lift up mine eyes unto the hills, from whence cometh my help." The journey up to Trion was a very happy experience.

But coming home was a different matter. My speech was entirely too long, and we were later starting back than we had expected to be. It was a dark, cloudy night, and we could see none of the beauties about us. Then, when both of us are away, no matter who we have sitting with the children, we think about them and are a little anxious.

So coming back we took the shortest way. I wanted to get the trip over as quickly as possible. It was not a pleasant drive.

So in the journey of life. For some it is an altogether happy experience. Every mile of the way brings new joys and thrills. But for some it is a dark, worried way, and the quicker it ends the better.

I have said privately to many people who are finding

life "not worth living," that if they will start walking God's way they will see a marvelous change.

To walk God's way you must surrender your will to His will. You must reach the point where you say completely, "Not my will but thine be done."

Reread the story of the Prodigal Son (Luke 15:11-24). The boy started out on his own. He left home to live as he pleased. The father did not go out to try to force him to come back. Instead, the father waited patiently for the boy to decide for himself. The boy experienced a lot of grief before he finally "came to himself." Then he was willing to come back to his father with the plea, "Make me . . ." He had reached the point where he was willing to put his life in his father's hands, and a new life became his.

Remember, God leads us a step at a time. So the important thing is to take the first step you can see on God's way and not worry about how or where you will end up.

Dr. Charles E. Jefferson used to tell a story about a young bear cub which was puzzled about how to walk. The little bear said to his mother, "Shall I move my right paw first or my left? Or shall I move my two front paws together and then the two back ones? Or the ones on the left side together then the ones on the right? Or should I try to move all four paws at the same time?"

I can see how the little bear would get confused. But the mother very wisely replied, "Stop thinking about it and just walk."

If we keep thinking about this and that problem, worrying about what might happen in the future, we get so mixed up that we get nowhere. But when one wholeheartedly begins to walk God's way as best he understands it, then he takes each step as God reveals it.

Then one begins to face the future with anticipation rather than with fear and apprehension. There is marvelous comfort in the fact that whatever may happen tomorrow it will be for the best, because God's way always leads to the best. This takes the dread and fear out of living and makes each new day a grand adventure.

A business man in Atlanta told me that he had not had time to go to church. In fact, he felt sufficient unto himself and did not need the help of God. But one week he had some serious trouble and the next Sunday night he did go to church. His heart was moved by the service, and when the invitation was given, he went forward and knelt at the altar, consecrating his life to God's way. He has been a happy man since.

Are You Lonely?

One of the things I miss most since moving to a big city is the privilege of speaking to everybody I meet.

I grew up in little towns in Georgia where we always spoke to each other. I tried to get acquainted even with the dogs of the town, because when you meet a little boy, if you know the name of his dog and ask about him, that little boy will be your friend for life.

Even now I catch myself speaking to people as I walk down Peachtree Street and find them looking at me as if I were a perfect idiot.

I was on a bus one day when a pretty girl in a nurse's uniform sat down beside me. Now, I like nurses—they are grand people. So I said to this girl, "What's your name?"

She looked at me as though I had shot her. But I explained that I had not been living here long and I just didn't know everybody. I told her who I was and she told me her name. Then she told me that she had moved here from a little town two years before and had been so lonely she could hardly stand it.

I was talking one day to a dear old lady who faces

that same loneliness. She had reared several children, but now they were scattered, her husband had died, and she lived alone.

She told me it wasn't so bad until she sat down to eat. She said that eating just by your lone self after having had a large family is hard to do. In fact, she is not as well as she might be, just because she isn't eating correctly, and said she had no incentive to cook a balanced meal just for herself.

On one occasion, after visiting a family in an apartment house, I was in no special hurry and decided to try a little experiment. There were sixteen apartments in that building and I decided to visit the people in every one, though I did not know any of them. So I knocked on every door.

In six of them nobody was at home. I had already visited in one, so that left nine. When someone in each of those nine opened the door, I simply said I was a preacher and thought I would just stop in to see them a few minutes. The cordial welcome I received in every instance really amazed me. And it seemed to me that every one of them appreciated my coming and was glad to talk to somebody.

Most people in Atlanta call WALnut 8550, the number that gives us the correct time. I know of one old lady in town who calls that number every night just before going to bed. Somebody asked her if she did not have a clock.

"Yes," she said, "I have a clock, but I call, not because I want to know the time, but just to hear somebody's voice before I go to bed."

A man told me recently how life had been with him since he retired. For forty-two years he had been on the job, and now had no job any more.

He had enough pension to live on, but he needed something to do. He had a small yard, but after a few weeks had done everything in it that needed doing. He watches for the mail man every morning, and he says he now reads carefully every circular he gets.

But when you are retired, even those who send out circulars drop your name, and he doesn't get much mail. He had looked forward to retiring and had worked for it, but now that it has come he is miserable.

Surely there must be an answer. The church can do a lot. We stress our youth programs, but we need more programs for those whose youth is gone. Other organizations could be doing a lot more to help. But the lonely person himself can find the answer if he will only take it. In the wisest book on human relations ever written there is this formula:

"He that loseth his life . . . shall find it."

Instead of thinking about yourself, realize that you are in the midst of many other people who are very lonely. Then set out to do something for a few of the others.

It will amaze you how grateful and responsive those you try to help will be, and when you see how you have helped, there will come a warm glow into your hearts that will be about the best feeling you have ever had.

You can never overcome this problem of loneliness by thinking about it. "He that loseth his life . . . shall find it."

One of the tragedies of a big city is that there are so

many people slowly starving to death. Not starving for physical food, because there are numerous agencies that will give hungry people something to eat, but starving for a little attention.

A girl telephoned me for an appointment. I could not see her that week, and suggested that we talk a few moments on the phone. She told me her story. When she was born her mother died. Her father died when she was two years old, and she was taken to live with some relatives who did not want her.

When she was fifteen she came to Atlanta and got a job in a big corporation. She has worked there for seventeen years, and all of those years she has lived in boarding houses. She told me, "I am now thirty-two years old, and I do not know what it means to be loved by even one person."

Certainly our Lord understands a hungry heart. One of the saddest stories I know is the story St. Luke tells about Jesus healing the ten lepers (17:11-19). He healed them all, but only one returned to thank Him. He expressed His disappointment when He said, "Were there not ten cleansed? but where are the nine?" He wanted no pay, but He did want the love and appreciation of his fellow men.

St. John gives us a scene in the Lord's life that reveals the same thing. John says, "From that time many of his disciples went back, and walked no more with him" (John 6:66). It is hard to have a friend walk out of your life. Jesus turned to the twelve disciples and almost wistfully said, "Will ye also go away?" There are times when all that matters is the love and loyalty of someone, without which life is pretty empty.

Deep in every heart is the yearning to be accepted, to be loved, and a feeling that one means something to somebody. But people do not express their appreciation very much. Most are like the nine whom Jesus healed. They just go on and forget you.

Samuel Leibowitz, now a famous judge but formerly a great criminal lawyer, saved seventy-eight persons from the electric chair. Yet not one of the seventy-eight ever bothered even to send him a word of thanks. Art King had a radio program called "Job Center of the Air." He got good jobs for 2,500 people, yet only ten ever bothered to thank him.

In his very first political speech, Abraham Lincoln said to the voters of Sagamon County, "I have no other ambition so great as that of being truly esteemed by my fellow men." Look into the hearts of most people and you will find their greatest desire is the same as was Lincoln's. And many feel they have missed it.

Well, many with hungry hearts give way to self-pity, become emotional invalids, and spend the rest of their lives bitterly nursing themselves. But others refuse to give up, and, instead, do something positive and constructive to meet their need.

A high-school girl was elected president of her class. Her father asked, "How did that happen?" She replied, "It did not happen, I happened it."

A year ago a lovely young woman came to see me with her problem: she wanted, above all things, to get married, and she did not even have a boy friend. She was very sorry for herself and wanted my sympathy. I began talking with her about how girls get boy friends, and we outlined a little plan of action. She put the plan to work, and a few weeks ago I stood at the altar of the church and watched her walk down the aisle in a lovely white dress.

It takes some planning and work, but there are lasting friendships waiting for anyone who will do his part. I have heard people say, "I do not have an enemy in the world," and it is true. Yet it may also be true that they do not have any friends, either. Many people have neither friends nor enemies. To have friends requires that you do the things that make friends. And what you need to do is expressed in this little poem.

If any little love of mine may make a life the brighter,
If any little song of mine may make the heart the lighter;
God help me speak the little word and take my bit of
singing,
And drop it in some lonely vale to set the echoes ringing.

If any little love of mine may make a life the sweeter;
If any little care of mine may make a friend's the fleeter;
If any little lift may ease the burden of another,
God give me love and care and strength to help my toiling
brother.

(Author Unknown)

The Prodigal Son had an older brother, who lived a morally decent life. He never committed the sins of his prodigal brother. But Jesus ends the story of the two boys with the prodigal at the father's table and the self-righteous older brother out in the darkness. Though the older brother stayed at home, worked, and lived an outwardly good life, Christ has not a kind word to say about him (Luke 15:11-32).

I can see several things wrong in him. (1) He refused to recognize his brotherhood. In complaining to the father he said, "This thy son." Gently the father corrects him with, "This thy brother," but the boy would have none of it. It is bad to go into the far country, but perhaps it is even worse to be one who does not care and is not anxious to welcome the prodigal home.

The news of the prodigal's wrong-doing must have come back. The father's heart was wounded, but he retained his faith in the boy, continued praying for him, and kept watching for his return. But the older brother probably spread the news even farther. I can hear him saying, "Did you hear about that fellow? Don't quote me, but this is what I heard . . . ," and off he would go with his self-righteous gossip. There are people who seem really to enjoy the fall of another.

(2) The fact that his brother did things he had not done gave the older son a false sense of moral superiority. Why do people talk about another who has fallen? It isn't because they are sorry for him. Rather does it give them a chance to boast. When we gossip, what we are really saying is, "See what that person has done. I have not done that, therefore I am better." Not being worth much themselves, they enjoy the failure of another.

Jesus told a story of two men who went to church to pray. One man looked around and picked out some who had failed and compared himself with them. Thus he prayed, "God, I thank thee that I am not as other men are." He had a good eye on himself, a bad eye on his fellow men, and no eye at all on God.

The other man prayed, "God be merciful to me a sinner." In commenting on the two Jesus said, "I tell you, this man went down to his house justified rather than the other: for every one that exalted himself shall be abased; and he that humbleth himself shall be exalted" (Luke 18:10-14).

Listen to the older brother: "Lo, these many years do I serve thee, neither transgressed I at any time thy commandment." That is nothing but self-righteous bragging, and the father is not pleased with it.

(3) It seems that the older son stayed at home just for what he could get out of it. He sees the banquet spread for the prodigal and he complains, "Thou never gavest me a kid, that I might make merry with my friends." Notice the pronouns he uses, "me," "I," "my." That shows whom he was thinking about. I suspect that he was a bit envious of the prodigal's life and would have enjoyed a taste of the "far country" himself, but he stayed at home because he felt it was the expedient thing to do.

(4) The prodigal committed sins of the flesh, which were bad and for which he suffered. But the elder brother committed sins of the spirit, which were worse.

For example, one can steal money and be sent to prison. But it is far worse for a bad temper to steal the peace and happiness of a home. One might set off a stick of dynamite under a church and he would be prosecuted for it. But it is a greater crime for an unbridled tongue or a sulky spirit to blast the brotherhood and fellowship of the church.

One boy sinned. He recognized his sin, repented of it, and started again in the right way. The other boy also sinned. But his self-righteous conceit blinded him to the need of repentance and change. He was good enough as he was.

So in the end the prodigal was at the father's table while the older brother was out in the darkness. When we think of the "lost son" let us remember which son it was who was lost.

There are many books on how to win friends, the art of popularity, and human relations in general, but by far the best thing ever written on such subjects is the twelfth chapter of Romans. Any person who learns and applies the principles listed there will never lack for friends. Today, I would like to list a few of them.

(1) "Not to think of himself more highly than he ought to think" (v. 3). The quickest pathway to unpopularity is conceit. However, that does not mean that we are to crawl in the dirt. Phillips Brooks once said: "The true way to be humble is to stand at your full height against some higher nature."

People sometimes say a nice word to me about my preaching, and I appreciate it, but I would never get conceited over it, because I have heard many of the really great preachers of our time. And when I hear one who is so far superior to me, and realize how far short I fall, it is hard not to be humble and do my very best at the same time.

The same principle can be applied in your life. Do your very best, but also remember how many others there are who are so much greater than you, and you will have no trouble observing this first rule of popularity.

(2) "We, being many, are one body" (v. 5). I am lifting out a phrase there but doing no violence to the meaning. This is simply saying that there are numerous people, and that it takes us all to make the world. It means to recognize that every person's place is important.

Once a pen remarked, "I am writing the book." But the ink replied, "I am writing a book. You could not make a mark if it were not for me." The paper replied, "But what could either of you do without me?" Then the dictionary said, "If I did not supply the words no book could be written." And all during the argument the author just smiled.

(3) "Abhor that which is evil; cleave to that which is good" (v. 9). The real basis of popularity is respect, and no person has either his own self-respect or the respect of others who refuses to stand for the good and against the evil. No person gains popularity by becoming cheap or smutty.

(4) "Patient in tribulation" (v. 12). Constant complaining and sympathy-seeking never wins friends. Every person has his sorrows, and it does not make him like you better for you to try to suggest that yours are the worst anyone has ever had.

There was an old man who was always thankful. He was struck down with a severe sickness of chills and fevers. A friend said, "I don't think you have anything to be thankful for now?" He replied, "Oh, yes, when I have the fever I am thankful for chills that cool me off, then I am thankful for the fever that warms me up again."

No matter how bad your trouble is, there is always some reason for gratitude. A man got both his feet cut off. However, he said his feet were always cold and he would not be bothered with cold feet again.

(5) "Bless them which persecute you. . . . Recompense to no man evil for evil. . . . Avenge not yourselves. . . . Overcome evil with good" (vs. 14, 17, 19, 21).

Little people are always afraid they won't get their rights, while a big person is always willing to surrender a few rights.

Once I was driving along the highway when, in attempting to pass a truck, another car almost ran into me head-on. I turned off into the ditch, and I am here to write these words because I was willing to surrender my rights at that time.

Jesus talked about "turning the other cheek," and while it seems impractical in a world like ours today, still it works for all who do.

There are at least ten other principles as important as these five I have mentioned in that same chapter. Read the twelfth chapter of Romans carefully every morning and every night for one month and you will see a distinct difference in your attitude toward other people and in their attitude toward you.

And notice one other thing. Paul said, "If it be possible . . . live peaceably with all men" (v. 18). He uses the word "if," indicating that there will be a few whom you cannot live peaceably with. Recognize that fact and concentrate on the vast majority of people whom you can get along with happily.

The doctor is called to prescribe for a group of sick

people. After examination, he discovers they are filled with poisons that will not only eventually destroy their bodies, but rob them of all the joy and peace of life, and eventually destroy their souls.

He discovers they are filled with the poisons of envy, jealousy, selfishness, and hate. Each one is thinking of himself as more important than any of his fellows. One says he is the finest public speaker. Another claims to be able to look into the future, while another feels he is better educated. Still another claims to do more for other people.

The wise doctor tells them that no matter what abilities they possess or what services they render, if their hearts are not filled with love they do not amount to anything. Then he analyzes his prescription, love. The doctor is St. Paul, and you can read all of this in I Corinthians 13.

Love is not a single thing, but really a composite of many things. (1) Love contains patience, "suffereth long." This is the attitude. To be patient means to possess endurance under stress or annoyance. Love works today while it waits for tomorrow.

On the desk of a very fine business man I saw this motto, "This, too, shall pass." He told me that the motto had saved him many times. No matter how bad the storm may be, if you are sure that one day it will blow out and the sun will shine again, you will never give up.

(2) "And is kind." That is the activity of love. Many years ago I learned a little verse that has been a constant inspiration to me:

So many gods, so many creeds, go many ways that
wind and wind;
When all this world needs, is just the art of being
kind.

A man once said about his sick wife, "There is nothing I would not do for her." One of the neighbors replied, "That is just the trouble, you have been doing nothing for her for forty years."

(3) Love "envieth not." As Henry Drummond, who wrote the greatest sermon on this chapter in existence, said, "This is love in competition with others." Envy leads to hate and hate destroys the soul. Love always congratulates.

(4) Love is humble "vaunteth not itself, is not puffed up." Love and conceit are contradictory terms. What God wants is men great enough to be small enough to be used. Love takes a towel, girds itself, and gets on its knees to do a menial task that lesser men are too big to do.

(5) "Doth not behave itself unseemly." Love is courteous. Love contains tact and good manners. The old, old saying is still true: "Politeness is to do and say the kindest thing in the kindest way." Love never wants to offend, it never demands its rights, it is respectful, and is ever mindful of the desires and comforts of others.

(6) "Seeketh not her own." The greatest verse in the Bible tells us: "For God so loved the world that he gave . . ." (John 3:16). Love is always more concerned with what it can give than with what it can get. Love seeks to minister rather than to be ministered unto. Love

understands that it is "not what we gain, but what we give, that measures the worth of the life we live."

(7) "Is not easily provoked." Love is good-tempered. Quick temper is a fault that many people brag about. They tell you about their temper as if it were a great asset. But it is no credit to be able to get angry.

There are two types of sins—the sins of the body and the sins of the disposition. Both are bad, but of the two, I would rather be in the company of some prodigal who had gone to the far country than with some elder brother who stayed at home and lived a moral life, yet had a bad disposition. Love knows how to keep certain emotions cool.

(8) "Thinketh no evil; rejoiceth not in iniquity." Love is not suspicious, and never accuses merely on rumor. Love believes the best of every person unless the contrary is proved. And even if some person does go wrong, love is not secretly glad and does not gossip about it.

Love bears its burdens with dignity, continues to believe, never loses hope, and endures to the end (v. 7).

Love is what the world needs and is what you need.

The visitor was very upset. In fact, she told me she was on the verge of a nervous breakdown. She had to force herself to eat, she had difficulty sleeping, and life for her, she said, was just not worth living.

Her husband had been unfaithful to her, but now he was deeply repentant. She did not want to break up her home, yet neither did she feel she could continue living with him. I told her she would have to forgive him and never mention it again. We talked about it, and finally she agreed to do so. We had a prayer together, in which she told God she had forgiven her husband and asked God to forgive him, also.

Then I said, "You must forgive that other woman." She bristled up and almost shouted, "That I will never do. I cannot, and, even if I could, I would not. She is a low, unmentionable creature, and as long as I live I will hate her. For me to forgive her is unthinkable and impossible."

I asked her if she had a television set. She had. I told her she also had one in her mind which was far more wonderful than one that can be bought. With your mental television you can see things that happened long ago. So I suggested that as I named some scenes of a certain drama she watch the pictures on the television screen of her mind. So I named the scenes as follows:

It is late at night as Jesus and eleven disciples are walking in the Garden of Gethsemane. They pause for a prayer together. Then Jesus and three of the men go on a little farther. He tells them to watch while He goes on a little farther by Himself. He is kneeling now by a large rock. She said she could see those scenes in her mind.

As He prays, we see a group of soldiers coming over the hill with torches. They come up to Him, and Judas betrays Him with a kiss. The soldiers roughly take the Lord and carry Him before the depraved Herod. There He is laughed at and scorned. Later, He is before the weak Pilate. His back is bared and before the howling mob He is lashed. Imagine anyone striking Christ!

Without even a trial, He is condemned to death and forced to carry a very heavy cross toward Calvary. The shouting mob lines the street. The cross is so heavy and He is in such a weakened condition that He faints under the load. A man has to help carry the cross, and they finally get to the top of the hill.

He is laid on the cross and nails are driven through His hands and feet. The cross is set in place. The soldiers gamble for His clothes, laugh at and mock Him. The physical agony is terrible, yet it isn't nearly so bad as the mental agony, the humiliation, and the bitter disappointment.

You see His lips moving. He is talking to God. You move closer and hear Him saying, "Father, forgive them."

I told this woman who said she could not forgive to keep those pictures on the screen of her mind while we looked briefly at another picture. "You," I said, "are the central character in this picture, and you are before the throne of God for your own judgment."

There all our past sins are brought before us. The idle words, the wrong deeds, the neglected opportunities, and even the wrong thoughts that have been in one's heart.

But you hear a voice saying, "If ye forgive men their trespasses, your heavenly Father will also forgive you: but if ye forgive not men their trespasses, neither will your Father forgive your trespasses" (Matthew 6:14,15).

Now, with the picture of Christ on the cross and also the picture of ourselves before the judgment bar of God, I asked the woman how she felt. Before she was harsh, but now she gently whispered, "I can forgive now." She did, and she left with a new song in her heart.

You can forgive, too.

How to Get What You Want

"Is there a something, a force, a factor, a power, a science —call it what you will—which a few people understand and use to overcome their difficulties and achieve outstanding success?" Claude M. Bristol asked that question and he answers it by saying, "Yes." He calls that something "The Magic of Believing."

Jesus said, "If ye have faith . . . nothing shall be impossible unto you" (Matthew 17:20). The author of Hebrews defines faith as "the substance of things hoped for, the evidence of things not seen" (11:1).

That is, when you picture something clearly in your mind and entirely give yourself to it, you can do even seemingly impossible things.

I was having dinner with a planter in the Mississippi delta. He was telling me about large numbers of migrant Mexican workers who came there to hoe and pick cotton. They live almost like animals, sleeping ten or twelve in one room, eat very crudely, and have nothing.

I asked, "What do they think about the life they live?" He said, "That's just it, they don't think."

The author of Hebrews in that eleventh chapter lists

a number of great people who applied the principles of faith and found them to work. For example, he cites Moses. For forty years he was a sheep herder. He had time to think as he watched the sheep.

On the screen of his mind Moses pictured the children of Israel. They were in bondage, but he pictured them as free people in the Promised Land, and later he did lead them out of Egypt, through the Red Sea, and to the very border of that Promised Land.

My wife often reminds me of our first date. It was one Sunday afternoon on the campus of Young Harris College. There were beautiful mountains all around, and the bright October sunshine made them glisten like great jewels. But I did not notice the mountains. She says I did not even notice her.

Instead, I spent the entire afternoon telling her that some day I would be the pastor of a church in a big city and that I would have a great Sunday-night service to which many people would come and would find God. I was only sixteen years old at the time, but the picture was clear in my mind.

That was a poor way to court. But I won the girl. And I got the church, too.

A young fellow came to my study and said, "I want you to pray for me." I asked what he wanted me to pray about. He told me he was in love with a certain girl and wanted to marry her, but was afraid she would decide on another boy.

I asked, "Do you really think she is the one for you?" A dreamy, far-away look came into his eyes, and he said, "If I don't get her I do not want any other. I just can't live without her." We prayed about it.

Because he believed so strongly, he courted her furiously. He didn't make much money, and he went without lunch three and four days in succession in order to be able to take her out to dinner on Saturday night. He gave up smoking so that he would have a little more money to spend on her.

I am happy to report that before long they will stand before the altar, and I will say, "What God hath joined together, let not man put asunder."

You see the principle. When you decide clearly and definitely what you want, then no sacrifice is too great as you put all of your powers into astounding results. It is this: Get perfectly relaxed and quiet in an attitude of prayer, and conceive of your mind as a blank motion picture screen.

Then flash on that screen the picture of the thing you want to accomplish. Look at the picture, then take it off. Then flash the picture back. Repeat that process, perhaps over a period of days, weeks or months, until every detail of it is clear and sharp.

That is a method of practicing faith—"the substance of things hoped for, the evidence of things not seen." And such faith will actually determine your life.

"Ye have not, because ye ask not." Those are the words of James (4:2) to the early Christians, but those same words apply to many people today who have little, but who could have so much.

Jesus emphasized the wisdom of asking over and over. He said: "And all things, whatsoever ye shall ask in prayer, believing, ye shall receive" (Matthew 21:22). That is a promise many believe too good to be true, yet those who try it find it to work.

I graduated from Young Harris Junior College in 1932. That was during the depression. A dollar would buy more then, but there were so few dollars it was hard to get one. I wanted to continue in college but did not have the money and could see no chance of making my way.

However, one day I wrote to Dr. H. N. Snyder, president of Wofford College, telling him my situation and asking him to open some way so that I could go to Wofford that year. Dr. Snyder had never heard of me, but I prayed as I wrote the letter, and I prayed while the letter was on the way. By return mail I received his letter telling me to come. My mother bought me some clothes and I went.

Several years ago I had an idea for a magazine for ministers. But it takes money to start publishing a magazine and I had none. However, I collected the facts about it and went to see a banker. I figured I would need $3,000, but knowing how bankers sometimes cut down your requests, I asked for $4,000. He said, "All right, we will be glad to let you have the money," and he deposited the full $4,000 to my account.

It is simply amazing what you can get when you ask for it. During the war, Miss Jane Frohman was in a plane wreck in the water off Lisbon, Portugal. She was taken to a hospital, and badly broken in body and spirit, she wanted to return home. However, there was absolutely no transportation available. But one day she wrote a simple letter to President Roosevelt telling him her situation and asking his help. She barely had time to pack her clothes to take advantage of the reservation he made available for her.

If there is something you want do not be afraid to ask for it. However, there are four principles we must observe.

(1) Decide exactly what you want before you ask. Then test your desire. Is it good for you? Are you ready for it now? Is it fair to all others concerned? Do you honestly feel it is according to God's will? If you can say yes to those four questions, then do not hesitate.

(2) Ask for it. Do not say, "Lord, you wouldn't do this for me, would you?" Take the positive approach, knowing that no matter how hopeless it seems there is always a way.

I read about a man who hit on a wonderful idea. Every night when he went to bed he would put his keys in one of his shoes. The next morning when he put on his shoes, his foot would hit those keys. He would take them out, and say this little prayer: "Lord, I know there is a key to every situation. May I not give up this day until I have found the keys that I need."

(3) Do what you can to answer your own requests. A girl in an office asked for a raise in salary. Her boss explained that he was paying her the top salary for a clerk, but that if she would go to a night school, learn shorthand and typing, then she would be in line for a fine increase in pay. But she was not willing to do that. She asked, but was not willing to help herself.

(4) Ask, believing. Most parents want the very best

for their children. Certainly God wants the best for us. Jesus said, "If ye then, being evil, know how to give good gifts unto your children, how much more shall your Father which is in heaven give good things to them that ask him?" (Matthew 7:11).

Concentrate on the goodness of God. Believe that God is your friend, that He hears your requests, and will answer them.

The most powerful force in this universe is the power of prayer, but many miss that power because they never really understand how to pray. Jesus said, "What things soever ye desire, when ye pray, believe that ye receive them, and ye shall have them" (Mark 11:24).

First, Christ puts your desire. It is amazing how many people there are who do not really know what they want. I have had many people come to me with a problem who for an hour could sit and tell me every detail of their problem. They had it fixed clearly in their minds.

Then I would ask what it would take to solve this or that problem, at which point most of them became very vague. We concentrate on our problems instead of on our desires, and thus we are defeated at the very outset. One of the first things we need to learn is the technique of visualization. It helps tremendously to write down exactly what our desires are. Do not deal in vague generalities, be specific and clear.

Many times the words of our prayer are in conflict with the real desires of our heart. We pray for one thing when really we want something else. The king in Shakespeare's Hamlet went to the church to pray, but his prayers were futile. In explaining it he said: "My words fly up, my thoughts stay below; words without thoughts never to heaven go."

"What things soever ye desire," Jesus said. What is the real and specific desire of your heart? That is the first step toward gaining prayer power.

Second, Jesus said, "Believe that ye receive them." The struggle in prayer is the struggle to believe. And what is it to believe? It means to see your desire as an accomplished fact in your mind. You must be able to visualize it though it has not actually come to pass. That is one important type of believing, and what, I think, Jesus meant in this statement.

Third, after you believe, that is, see your desire accomplished in your mind, then comes the next step to prayer power: "All things are possible to him that believeth" (Mark 9:23). Jesus does not say all things are actual. He says, possible. As you believe, the word "impossible" gradually drops out of your thinking, and, instead, hope and faith come in. You stop your negative thinking and begin to see solutions.

In my own church we have a little theme song that we sing every Sunday night just before the prayer. Hundreds of people have told me how that short chorus has wonderfully blessed their lives and changed their attitudes. It is, "Only believe, only believe; all things are possible, only believe." It is simple, yet profound and wonderful.

When we believe, then our prayer is already answered in our minds. Maybe not actually in our lives, but our prayer has come within the realm of possibility.

Fourth, we realize, however, our own weakness and inability actually to accomplish our real desires. Then we remember that Jesus said, "The things which are impossible with men are possible with God" (Luke 18:27). Then we begin to look to God for the strength and help we lack. If we were strong enough by ourselves we would not need prayer power. So we begin to recognize our need of God. And at the same time we recognize the strength and power of God.

Fifth, now comes the final step of prayer power. We surrender our life to God and His will so that His power may flow in and through us. The result of our prayer is not what we may have persuaded God to do, but rather what God can work in us to the accomplishment of our highest purposes and greatest needs and desires.

In this final step to prayer power, we become willing to surrender anything and everything in life that is inconsistent with the will and spirit of God, and we begin to say:

> Have Thine own way, Lord, have Thine own way.
> Thou art the potter, I am the clay.
> Mold me and make me after Thy will,
> While I am waiting, yielded and still.

Those are the five steps to prayer power.

Someone has said that the three steps to success are these: (1) visualize, (2) "prayerize," (3) "actionize." The teachings of Jesus certainly confirm that. For example, in Mark 11:24 Jesus said, "What things so ever ye desire, when ye pray, believe that ye receive them, and ye shall have them."

We all wish for things we do not have, but sometimes we feel a bit guilty because we think it is selfish to wish and, therefore, wrong. But actually Jesus teaches us the opposite.

"What things soever ye desire," He said. He was not rebuking us for wishing, rather was He encouraging us to wish. In fact, wishing is a form of faith. Hebrews 11:1 tell us, "Now faith is the substance of things hoped for."

In his book, *The Keys to the Kingdom,* A. J. Cronin said, "Hell is the place where one has ceased to hope." Hoping and wishing are so near the same thing that I cannot tell them apart. So, actually, wishing is one of the finest things we can do.

The first step is to visualize (wish for) clearly the things we really want.

Then "prayerize." In its deepest meaning, prayer is not asking for something, rather it is a committing of our lives to God. It is fellowship with God.

After I had talked about this on the radio one Sunday, a man told me that he had desired some things and had been bitterly disappointed. He said that my "theories" did not work. I said, "I want to ask you two questions:

"First, what are you doing with what you do have?" There are two principles involved in that question. One, it is possible to think so much of what we want that we forget what we have. It often happens that most of our wishes do come to pass and we fail to recognize the fact.

For example, I asked this man what his greatest desires were twenty years ago. He said he had wanted a wife, a home with children, and a job so that he could support them. I asked if that wish had come true, and he said it had. I suggested that instead of being bitter about some disappointments, he might, instead, be thanking God for giving him, perhaps, the great desires of his heart.

A second principle to keep in mind is that God may be unwilling to trust us with any more than we have because we have misused what He had already given us. I said to this man that he had wanted a home and a job, and that now I wanted to know if he had been the husband and father he should have been and had done his best on the job he had.

My second question to him was: "Is your life committed to the will of God?" God will help us only so long as we are following His way and will.

A completely dedicated life develops abilities and strengths that one never possessed before. Notice these words: "As many as received him, to them gave he power" (John 1:12). I am lifting just a phrase out of the entire verse but doing no violence to the meaning, because it is a demonstrable fact that when one puts his faith in Christ he gains a marvelous new power.

The third step is "actionize," that is, begin doing all you can. The second oldest college in America is William and Mary, Williamsburg, Virginia. It is today one of our most honored institutions. However, in 1881, as a result of the financial catastrophe which resulted from the War Between the States, William and Mary was closed.

It probably would have remained closed but for the faith of its president, Dr. Benjamin Ewell. Every morning for seven years he rang the old college bell. That is about all he could do, but he did that. And one great day William and Mary was reopened.

Visualize—"prayerize"—"actionize," and your wishes will come true.

The "What-Are-You-Going-to-Do" Question

Some people think harmlessness is holiness. They think the only requirement for goodness is not being bad. They take great pride in the sins they do not commit and they are satisfied because of the harm they are not doing.

Jesus told about a man who drove an evil spirit out of his life. The man probably boasted that he had overcome this evil thing and felt quite complacent and pleased with himself. But one day the evil came back and looked into the man's life and found nothing there to take his place.

So the spirit went out and found seven other spirits even worse than himself, and they all moved into the man's life. As a result, the man ended up in a worse state (Matthew 13:43-45).

In Jesus' day the Pharisees had this negative approach. For example, they had a long list of things one could not do on the Sabbath. Jesus violated some of their laws and they severely condemned Him. In reply, Jesus simply said, "Is it lawful on the Sabbath days to do good?" (Luke 6:9).

That is, instead of talking so much about what we should not do on Sunday, let us begin concentrating on what we should do and go to work on that. We will come out much better that way.

I have a close friend who became the pastor of some little country churches. The preacher before him had told the people of their sins in emphatic language. He was one of those "fearless" preachers, but the little churches had about died under his ministry.

My friend took a different approach. His very first sermon was on the text, "Whosoever heareth these sayings of mine, and doeth them" (Matthew 7:24). He "accentuated the positive." At the close of his sermon he passed out sheets of paper on which were written four questions:

(1) What are you going to do this month to make you a better Christian? He got such answers as, "I am going to read the Gospel of Matthew," "I am going to speak kindly to every person I meet," etc.

(2) "What are you going to do this month to make your home happier?" One listed daily family prayers, another said he would clean up his yards and make them look better. One man would not say, but at the end of the month he told the minister to come around and see. It was a kitchen sink. He explained that his wife had always "toted" water from the spring on the hill. During the month he had run a pipe from the spring into the kitchen, and now the wife had all the water she needed. As a result, she could rest more and feel happier.

(3) Instead of complaining about their lack of support of the church, the minister asked, "What are you going to do this month to make your church better?"

They listed such things as regular attendance, inviting others, contributing more, etc. One man said he would try to sing better.

(4) What are you going to do this month to help your community? Some of the answers were: "I am going to work for better recreational facilities for the young people," "I am going to work for community co-operation," etc.

Every month the minister put before the people a series of "What-are-you-going-to-do" questions. He had very little to say about their sins. But at the end of the year the congregations of the little churches had more than doubled and for the first time these people realized something of the joy and thrill of positive Christian living.

You may be interested in a garden. You can select a plot of ground, dig up every weed, and get the plot as clean as a highway. But you never will have a garden until you get some flowers or vegetables growing there. We need to remember that the value of a rose bush is measured, not by the number of thorns it does not have, but rather by the number of roses it does have.

So if you are looking for a happier and richer life make a list of "What-am-I-going-to-do?" questions and get started. Try the positive approach and see how much better it is that way.

For some time I had felt an impulse to bake a cake. I had never baked one, but the recipes seemed so simple that I wanted to prove to my wife how easy cooking really is. So I took the cook book down and selected a recipe that suited me, chose the proper pans and ingredients, and went to work.

Some three hours later I sadly realized that baking a cake requires a wonderful talent, one that the Lord had not bestowed on me. There are many other talents. Cheerfulness is a talent. It is good to be able to write a poem, but it is better to be able to live a poem. Some people seem to have been born with a talent to be happy and to make others feel happy.

One of the finest talents is the ability to be a friend. To be able to overlook faults in others, to enter into the sorrows and joys of others with a sympathetic heart and to be loyal and true no matter what happens. To be able to suffer triumphantly is another fine talent.

When we hear the word "talent" we usually think of the ability to play a piano, make a speech, sing a song, or to be brilliant at something else. But the far more important talents are in certain qualities of character that mean so much to the people around us.

Jesus told a story about a man who gave his servants some talents. To one he gave five, to another two, and to another one. Two of the men used their talents, but the third man did nothing with his. When the master came home, he was very complimentary to the two and very harsh with the third (Matthew 25:14-30).

In that story we are taught that we are not equally talented. We are not born equal. Some are born with strong bodies, while others will have weak bodies all their lives. Some are born with more mental capacity than others. I think some people inherit certain moral and spiritual abilities that make it easier for them to live right than others.

Then we do not have equal opportunities to use our

talents. Here are two farmers. One has rich bottom land and he makes seventy-five bushels of corn per acre. Another farmer works just as hard, but his is much poorer land, and he make only twenty-five bushels per acre. So in life. Some have much richer opportunities of service.

But Jesus severely condemned the man with one talent. Not because he could not do what the others could do, but rather because he did not do what he could do. Now, the question I am most interested in here is: Why did not this man use the talent he had? The man himself answers that. He says, "I was afraid."

Day after day, I see people who are failing miserably because fear has put its paralyzing hand on their lives. What was the one-talent man afraid of? I think it was mainly one thing—he was afraid he could not be as outstanding as the others, so he just did nothing.

The root of that sort of fear is a silly and foolish pride. The good Lord invested certain talents in each of us, and He is not the least concerned with what we do as compared with what some other people do. But He is tremendously concerned with the return He receives on His investment in each of us.

In his poem, "The Day and The Work," Edwin Markham says it well:

There is waiting a work, where only your hands can avail;
And if you falter, a chord in the music will fail.

My middle name is "Livingstone." My father named me after the great missionary, and because of that fact I have read all I could find on his life. When Livingstone's body lay in Westminster Abbey a big African Negro stood at the head of the casket. He was the one who brought the body out of the jungle. And he insisted that he remain with it until it was buried.

Livingstone was a five-talent man. He possessed medical skill, a brilliant mind, charm of personality, a vision of the Dark Continent lighted by Christ, and an intense devotion to duty.

In contrast, the Negro was just one step removed from the savage. A strong body was about all he had. But in God's sight the two men were and are equal. Both were faithful to the best that was within them.

"Thou hast been faithful," Jesus said to the ones who used their talents. And "being faithful" is what counts.

One of the finest stories I know came out of the life of Dr. Gunsaulus, the famous Chicago preacher of some years ago. One Saturday morning, while he was in his study writing a sermon, his nephew came in. The boy was a fine athlete about twenty-five years old, but he had never been quite able to find himself.

He noticed his uncle's sermon text, "For this cause came I into the world" (John 18:37). That is a statement of Jesus to Pilate. The boy said, "Uncle, I wish I knew why I was born." That gave the preacher a chance to say a few words to him about life, and soon the boy went on his way.

While he was walking down the street he heard the fire engines. He noticed that the old Iroquois Theater was burning. In that fire more than five hundred people lost their lives. The boy rushed over, and when he arrived he saw a number of people gathered around a balcony window.

Quickly he found a heavy plank, climbed on the building next to the theater and laid the plank across to that window. Then he stood in the window and helped many people across to safety. However, while he was working, a heavy timber fell on him and knocked him to the pavement below. Just before he died his uncle got to him and said, "Now you know why you were born. You were born to save those people."

The curtain drops on the story there. But several years later Dr. Gunsaulus was traveling in Europe. One night he met a man in a hotel lobby, and in the ensuing conversation the preacher mentioned he was from Chicago, when the other man suddenly became hysterical and began to mutter something over and over. Another man came over and led him away.

Later Dr. Gunsaulus asked the third man what had caused the distressing scene. The man said it was a very sad case. He told Dr. Gunsaulus that his new acquaintance was in Chicago one Saturday and went to the old Iroquois Theater. The theater caught fire but this man got out. However, to get out, he had to climb over many screaming and fear-crazed people.

Though he himself was not harmed he became insane thinking about the experience. As a result, he fell into the habit of saying over and over, "I saved nobody but myself. I saved nobody but myself."

I speak at numerous banquets of various types. I notice that when I tell a joke people will laugh, if I talk about the news of the day, people are interested. But when I begin talking about Jesus, a strange tenderness comes over their faces.

Why do people love Him so? I think Jesus' critics gave us the answer. As Jesus was dying on the cross, a man was heard to say, "He saved others; himself he cannot save" (Matthew 27:42). That was meant to be a criticism of Christ, but in reality it was the greatest tribute that could have been paid Him.

We are born with two instincts: hunger and the fear of falling. Even as tiny babies our first thoughts are concerned with satisfying our hunger and holding on to someone. And those are the first thoughts of many people all the way through their lives. That is the reason so very few people ever rise to greatness. They never save anybody but themselves.

Recently I flew down the Mississippi for about a hundred miles. It was a beautiful moonlight night, and the great river below our plane looked like a flowing silver ribbon as the soft beams of the moon played on it.

It gave me a tremendous thrill to watch the river, the greatest in the world. For centuries it has been giving all that it has. It freely pours all of its water into the big Gulf of Mexico.

But suppose the Mississippi decided it could not afford to give so freely, that, instead, it began to hold back for fear it would run dry. Then it would cease to be a river and become a swamp. As a swamp it would be an ugly thing and a breeder of evil.

It gives all it has, but it has not run dry. God takes care of the river. He causes the sun to draw the water out of the gulf into clouds, the winds carry the clouds back up the river, and the clouds pour the water back. What the river gives, it gets back.

One of the unexplainable but true mysteries of life is that you never lose what you give. The wisest man who ever walked on this earth said, "He that loseth his life for my sake shall find it" (Matthew 10:39). No person ever really begins to live until he finds something big enough to give himself to.

It was one night when we were sitting around the fireside. Our father was in one of those mellow moods that always called for stories. He told us this story but that one time, yet I think it was his favorite of all the boyhood experiences he used to tell us about.

He grew up in the Loudsville community, in White County, Georgia. The family had very little money then, but they didn't need much. Life was simple and they lived a rather secluded life.

It was the Christmas Eve when he was seven years old. His father was going to drive to Cleveland and told him he could go along. Just before they got to Cleveland his father handed him a dime.

It was the first dime my father ever had, and he could spend it just as he liked. When they got to town he began looking in the stores for something he could buy. He said he could have spent a peck of dimes had he had them. He saw some oranges—the first he had ever seen. He wondered how an orange tasted. He saw a big red tablecloth with part of the Constitution of the United States printed on it. He wanted one of those. There were toys, red-striped candy, and so many other things that he was still trying to decide when dinner time came. He went back to the wagon and he and his father ate their dinner.

Then he hurried back to a store, trying to decide what

he most wanted to buy with the first dime he had ever had. Finally it was time to go home. He made a decision, put the package in his pocket, and ran to the wagon.

While they were riding along home, he pulled the package out of his pocket. It was a huge red handkerchief. Then he looked up at his father, handed it to him, and said, "I bought you a Christmas present."

All the remainder of his life I think my father got more joy out of giving his dime back to the father who gave it to him than he would have received from anything he could have bought for himself.

This is a great big world and there are so many ways I can spend my little life. In fact, there are so many ways I would like to spend it, it is hard to know just what to do. I can spend it all just for myself.

The very best and biggest way I can invest the life I have is to give it back to the Father who gave it to me. In that way I am sure to get more out of it.

It is true for all of us.

Let Christ Make You

He was born in a tiny village of an important little country. During the first thirty years of His life we have only one brief glimpse of Him. Then for three short years He served as a minister. He spoke in simple language, healed the sick and brought hope to sinners. A few people followed and learned from Him.

When He was about thirty-three, He was crucified and after three days He rose from the dead. His few followers began to tell others about Him and every year more people have heard about Him and have been drawn to Him. And now He has more followers than any person who has ever lived on this earth.

What is the explanation of His continuing and growing power? We cannot explain Him in human terms. There have been many good and great men, but none of them has become such an object of worship as has Jesus Christ. There is something eternally different about Him, and many can sing: "I know not how that Bethlehem's babe could in the Godhead be; I only know the manger child has brought God's life to me."

I preach an average of more than 400 sermons a

year. That is many more sermons than there are days in a year. It seems that the more one preaches the easier it would be, but, really, with every sermon it gets harder, and I will tell you why. When a young preacher starts out, he is anxious to impress people with his knowledge and abilities.

But as the years come along you get to know the needs of a lot of people. You soon become aware of your own weaknesses and inability to help and you become less interested in trying to impress people with yourself and vastly more interested in trying to impress people with the One who can help. But He is so wonderful and your words are so weak that you close every sermon with disappointment in your heart.

St. Paul felt this same disappointment with his own preaching. What a brilliant and eloquent preacher Paul was, yet after telling about Christ as best he could, he still realized that he had not told half the story. So Paul added, "Eye hath not seen, nor ear heard, neither have entered into the heart of man, the things which God hath prepared for them that love him" (I Corinthians 2:9). That is to say, you never saw anything, heard anything or even imagined anything so wonderful as what happens to you when you completely love Christ and trust Him with all your heart. No preacher can express in words what Christ can do for a human life. But the reason more and more people worship Him is because He is One who can save, and He is the only One.

We know how He took a spineless man and made a Simon Peter out of Him, changed a greedy tax collector into a Matthew, transformed a hotheaded John into an apostle of love, lifted a woman out of the gutter and made her a lovely Mary Magdalene, struck down a narrow, bigoted Saul and raised him a St. Paul, fell in step with two hopeless disciples on the road to Emmaus and made their hearts burn within them. But the reason He is still conquering today is because He is still changing people.

One of the happiest young ladies I know in Atlanta today was a street-walker a year ago. I know a man who was drunk for a week last Christmas. After it was over, he was bitterly ashamed and his family was very hurt and disappointed, but he will be sober this year and things will be different at his house.

There is a mother in Atlanta who a year ago was crushed and bitter with grief because of the death of a loved one, but today she is happy. I could name many whose lives were wrecked by worry, fear, anxiety or tension, but today they know a new peace. Somehow, belief in Him caused a change in their hearts.

Sometime ago I said in a newspaper column that if you will read the Gospel of Matthew ten times, slowly and deliberately, it will change your life. Since then I have received letters from many people telling me of wonderful things that have come into their lives as a result of reading Matthew's gospel. One man told me that after the first reading he felt he had gotten very little from it. The fifth reading meant a lot to him, but as he finished it for the tenth time he found something that he never knew existed.

The point is, as one becomes intimately acquainted with Christ, he becomes conquered by Christ and begins to know the truth of Christ's words, "Come ye after me and I will make you . . ."

In my pastoral duties I see people every week for whom life has not been too good. I hear intimate details of disappointments, broken hearts, pains of every sort. I talk with many who are bitter, frustrated, and ready to give up.

Many have told me they were contemplating suicide and during the past two or three years, I have known of at least five who took their lives after talking with me. On the other hand, I can name perhaps fifty whose minds I have been able to change. No doctor wins every time.

The one thing I have to offer people is a Christ who knows what a hard time is. We have made Him a Christ of stained-glass windows, of sweet sentiments and fine hymns. But in the days of His flesh, he was the Christ of life that was hard and disappointing. Certainly He understands any person who is having a hard time.

Look at the home in which He lived. In one of His stories He tells about how the candle lighted the whole house (Matthew 5:15). He was probably talking from personal experience, describing the house He had lived in. If one candle would light the house it had to be only one room.

One of my recent visitors has the habit of getting drunk every week end. I asked about his circumstances and found that he lives in a one-room efficiency apartment. He and his wife have three little children, and, to cap the climax, his mother-in-law lives with them. The poor fellow just couldn't stand all the noise and confusion.

Being the oldest of eight children, Jesus had to drop

out of school when His father died in order to make a living for the others. He knows what some of our boys are having to go through now, their careers interrupted because of the war. Jesus was thirty before he He could get started in His life's work.

He talks about clothes that were patched and then repatched. That is, the patches were patched. When He talks about food, it is usually fish and bread, the food of the poor. Jesus personally knew very few of the luxuries of life. He knew what it was to have a hard time.

However, His life is a shining example of the words of St. Paul, "All things work together for good to them that love God" (Romans 8:28).

Because of His own poverty He could preach to the common people, and they heard Him gladly (Mark 12:37). He stood on the same level with people who needed help and because He could help them, He won them, and later these same common people spread His name over all the earth.

Early in life He learned about children, and when His disciples were turning children away, Jesus said, "Suffer little children . . . to come unto me" (Matthew 19:14). And through the stream of Christianity, mercy and love for little children have flowed. Our little children sing with assurance, "Jesus loves me, this I know."

The difficulties of that small, congested home prepared Him for His place as head of the family of God. When He saw His disciples—older children—fussing and complaining, He did not lose faith in them. He knew that even children of the same family have their little quarrels. Today He understands why we have so many different denominations, and I am sure He is not too displeased with His children fussing a little among themselves from time to time.

When He was a boy He worked with His father, but His father died, and as a young man Jesus must have missed His father terribly. But as He thought of His own father and as He thought of God, a truth of tremendous import burst upon Him. God is a father! Jesus was the first to teach us that.

At the age of only thirty-three He faced His death. He was so young to die. There was so much He wanted to do. But even on the cross He still kept His faith. He turned His face upward and said, "Father, into thy hands I commend my spirit" (Luke 23:46).

Even the cross worked out for good. Today it is embedded in the hearts of millions and it is slowly redeeming the world.

I like to work with a Christ like Him.

In one of my newspaper columns I offered to give a small copy of Warner Sallman's portrait of Christ to all who requested it. In answer to the requests, I sent out a hundred thousand copies. I wish every person had one and would study it every day. It will marvelously influence a mind and a life.

Mr. Sallman grew up in a Christian home and went to Sunday school. There he got Bible picture cards, which stirred in him a desire to be an artist. Later, while attending Bible School, he met a challenge. The dean told him the world needed a picture of Christ that was manly instead of effeminate.

Did He not work in a carpenter shop, go forty days

without food, sleep under the stars, preach in the desert, walk long distances and drive the money changers out of the Temple? Surely he was rugged and strong.

This thought burned itself into the mind of Sallman. Later he became art editor of a religious magazine, *The Covenant Companion*. He was assigned to paint the cover page for the February, 1924, issue. He said:

> I wanted to have something there that would be a challenge to young people. I was stumped. I couldn't think of anything up to the day of the deadline. I worked late that evening in my studio, but nothing seemed to strike a spark. I went to bed but could not sleep.
>
> Finally, about two o'clock in the morning, I had a visual picturization of the head of Christ, so clear and definite I could almost see it on paper. I immediately went to my studio and made a small thumbnail sketch of it, completed it in charcoal the next day, and submitted it just in time for the deadline, about 4:30 in the afternoon.

But the picture received very little notice until about ten years later. Dr. John Timothy Stone of the McCormick Theological Seminary in Chicago, told his students to go out and search the art shops and bring in the best picture of Christ they could find. After three months' searching, they brought in many pictures and Mr. Sallman's was voted the best.

In 1940 Mr. Sallman painted it in colors, and today it is by far the most popular portrait of Christ we have.

As you look at the picture you will first notice the eyes. Oh, what eyes Jesus had! Long years after, when the Gospel writers came to write of Him, they could not forget those eyes. Sometimes His eyes flashed with merriment, sometimes they were dim with tears. At times they melted in tenderness, and at other times they hardened like steel and were filled with stern rebuke.

As you study His face you will see it is a happy face. He is not frowning or scowling. He was filled with joy. "Be of good cheer," He said again and again. Some religions seek to take all the joy out of life, but not the religion of Jesus.

His face is vivid and vital. He has no sallow complexion. He is not weak and sickly. His face is deeply tanned by the wind and sun of outdoor life. He is tremendously alive. So alive was He that His very looks caused people to think of living forever.

His face is tender and sympathetic. Little children wanted to sit in His lap, a sick woman wanted to touch the hem of His garment, a man whose child was dying wanted Him to come to his home. The poor and the outcast felt comfortable in His presence. He was concerned with the problems of ordinary people, and He gave them His time and help.

After His resurrection, every appearance He made was to those who were troubled in heart: Mary weeping by the tomb, the friends on the road to Emmaus who had lost hope, the disciples trembling with fear, Thomas who doubted, and again to the disciples when they had failed.

Above all, His face is steadfast. The verse Mr. Sallman had in mind when he painted this picture was Luke 9:51, "He steadfastly set his face to go to Jerusalem." He could make a decision.

If you will keep this portrait in your billfold, it will have a strange and wonderful influence on your life. Jesus said, "Come ye after me and I will make you . . ." and truly He will.

Some letters ask about hell. There are many things to be said about it. To begin with, sin is black and ugly. It is the most terrible thing in the universe. I think one of the major sins of our generation is that so many people are making light of sin.

Sometimes we are told that our sins are not so serious. But they are serious enough to put the Son of God on the Cross. Christ is being crucified anew by my sins and your sins.

Though Christ is the supreme revelation of the love of God, the most terrible things ever said about sin fell from His lips. He told about the door being shut (Matthew 25:10). He said, "The Son of man shall send forth his angels, and they shall gather out of his kingdom all things that offend, and them which do iniquity; and shall cast them into a furnace of fire; there shall be wailing and gnashing of teeth (Matthew 13:41,42).

One need not go further than his own conscience to know that sin brings punishment. And we cannot escape that punishment by moving to the other side of the Mississippi river or to the other side of the world, or even to the other side of life. The Bible says, "Be not deceived; God is not mocked; for whatsoever a man soweth, that shall he also reap" (Galatians 6:7).

We know that hell is a place of remorse. In the story of the rich man and Lazarus (Luke 16:19,31) Abraham said to the man in hell, "Son, remember." I sometimes preach a sermon on the three memories: The memory that prevents, "Remember now Thy creator in the days of thy youth" (Ecclesiastes 12:1); the memory that saves, "And Peter remembered" (Luke 22:61); and the memory that curses, "Son, remember."

The memory in hell is a cursed memory. In describing the memory of hell Charles William Stubbs said: "The ghost of forgotten actions came floating before my sight, and the things that I thought were dead things were alive with a terrible might; and the vision of all my past life was an awful thing to face, alone with my conscience sitting in that solemn silent place."

Hell is a place where there are no good things. There are no flowers there, no trees, no sunsets. Never is a kind word spoken there. There are no friendships there because there is no love there.

Nearly every town has a dumping place somewhere on its outskirts. Nobody wants to live close to the city dump. It is where the useless, unusable, no-account things are thrown. The trash of the city is put there to be burned.

Hell is the dumping ground of the universe. There is nobody there but those who are not fit for the city of God. The useless people, the "no-account" people, the trash of the universe. I think often of St. John being exiled on Patmos. There were many ways in which it was punishment to him, but I have an idea that the severest punishment of all was the people he had to associate with in that prison, where the worst of the empire were dumped.

There are many other things I could say about hell, but in my own ministry I am much more concerned about another side. One night I was to preach at a country church. I had never been there before, and was not sure of the way. I came to a fork of the road, and had no idea which way to turn.

I asked a man to direct me. Now, he might have stood there for an hour telling me reasons why I should not take the wrong road. He might have told me that the wrong road was rough, rocky, and hard to travel. He might have spent a long time telling me that it was a dead-end road, that I would eventually get to where it would be too narrow for me to turn round to come back and that, finally, I would be lost. But he didn't have to indulge in any such harangue. He told me which road to take. I followed it and reached my destination.

Jesus said to one who was confused, "I am the way" (John 14:6). The business of the Christians is to show Him to the world. As we concentrate on Christ, commit our lives to Him and follow His way. He will save us not only from something but also to something.

One day during his reign King Edward VIII of England, who was especially concerned about social conditions, decided to visit some of the homes in a slum section on the water front where he was to christen a ship. He stopped first at a house in which lived one of the most disreputable men in the area. He had become a social outcast. Hearing a knock on his door, he shouted in a gruff voice, "Who is it?" The answer came back, "I am your king. May I come in?" Thinking it was a cruel joke, the man refused to open the door. The king, a gentleman who respected the rights of a man in his own household, would not force his way in, so he turned and left. And this poor man missed seeing his king.

St. John tells us that the King of kings and Lord of

lords comes to the door of each of us. He says, "Behold, I stand at the door and knock; if any man hear my voice, and open the door, I will come in to him, and will sup with him, and he with me" (Revelation 3:20). What a tragedy for one to fail to open the door.

Jesus comes knocking at our heart's door in many ways. He knocks through our failures. Simon Peter, for example, never really opened his life to Christ until he had failed. He was too self-sufficient. But one morning, after a shameful failure, he heard the gentle knocking as Jesus quietly said, "Simon, Simon, lovest thou me?"

Sometimes we are so proud and pleased and filled with ourselves that we have no room for Him. Then perhaps our health fails, or we lose our possessions or job, or one of the children goes astray, or our home is broken up, and we are self-sufficient no longer. Then we might hear His knocking.

He knocks through our sorrows. Many people have told me that in the midst of a deep sorrow they felt the presence and power of God in a very special way. There is a little chorus that expresses it: "Just when I need Him most, Jesus is near to comfort and cheer."

He knocks through a vision of our better selves and our sense of inadequacy. We become disgusted and ashamed of the life we have been living. We come to realize we are made for a better way. But our efforts to change ourselves seem hopeless and futile. Then we hear His knock as He says, "Come ye after me and I will make you . . ."

He knocks through the lives of others. When we come in contact with some person bigger and greater than ourselves we are inspired and strengthened. It may be the gentle goodness of a mother or the manhood of a father. It may be some person we know or a great life of history.

Christ also knocks through the lives of others in a negative way. I am sure that Judas has caused many to be loyal. When we see one who has fallen we realize that we, too, might fall.

Isaiah heard the call of God through a realization of the needs of others. God gave Isaiah a vision of a needy, unclean world, and asked, "Whom shall I send, and who will go for us?" (Isaiah 6:1-8). As Isaiah realized that he could help to meet that need he opened his heart to the knocking.

There are other ways in which Jesus knocks: through the study of His work, the memories of a better yesterday, the voice of a church service or the direct word of a friend. He knocks through the voice of conscience and sometimes through a special moving of His spirit.

Once I was pastor of a small church which was having a hard time raising money for missions. I announced at the morning service that I would come around that afternoon and collect the money. As I walked up the steps of one house, I saw the man inside. I knocked long and loud, but he would not open the door. He would have been glad for me to visit him, but he knew that to open the door that day would cost him something. So with some of us. To open our heart's door to Christ may cost us something. But to have Him is worth all the cost.

He is knocking at your door.

There is a song which runs: "I can tell you now the

time; I can take you to the place where the Lord saved me by His wonderful grace." A lot of people can honestly sing that. St. Paul could have sung it.

Paul's experience is recorded in Acts 9. So long as he lived he could tell how that on a certain day, at a certain spot on the road to Damascus, he found Christ and was converted. It was a climactic, overwhelming experience. Many people know the place and the hour they were converted.

But there are many more people who have had a much better Christian experience than even St. Paul had, yet are confused about it because they cannot give the exact hour and place. There is the experience of Timothy that Paul himself certainly recognized as valid.

Paul said to Timothy: "From a child thou hast known the holy scriptures which are able to make thee wise unto salvation" (II Timothy 3:15). Timothy grew up in a Christian home. He went to Sunday school and church all his life. The great Dr. Horace Bushnell said, "A child should grow up feeling he is a Christian and never knowing himself to be anything else." Timothy was one who did.

Dr. Clovis Chappell has pointed out the different ways horses are broken. Out West, a colt is turned loose on the wide prairies and it literally goes wild. Later, when the horse has grown enough, he is brought into a corral, a heavy saddle is slapped on his back, and a cowboy mounts. The horse kicks and bucks, but as long as he lives he will know that on a certain day, in a certain corral, he was broken.

But that is not the way the thoroughbreds of Kentucky are broken. In the first place, they are never allowed to run wild. From the day the thoroughbred is born he is nurtured and cared for. Soon the trainer will put a light bridle on him and lead him around. He later puts a blanket across his back and leads him around. As the horse grows, the weight on his back is increased. And one day the trainer will ride him.

The horse will not jump or buck. It is all right for someone to ride him. And we know that that horse is just as well broken as the wild West horse. Yet when was he broken? No one can say when, because it was a gradual and natural process.

I have three children. Every day since they were born my wife and I have prayed for them and with them. Each was dedicated and baptized at the altar of the church when only a few weeks old. As soon as they were able to learn they were taught to pray, "Now I lay me down to sleep . . . ," and each prays every night.

The stories of Jesus have been read and told to them over and over. Since they could walk, they have been in Sunday school. The first song they learned was, "Jesus loves me, this I know . . ." They have been taught the difference between right and wrong.

I know my children are Christians, yet they do not know when they became Christians. And I also know that so long as they stay on the pathway on which they were, it will be utterly impossible for them to have an experience like the one St. Paul had. There are many people who have had Timothy's experience.

Then there is the type of experience that Zacchæus had (Luke 19:9). He was a mean, selfish, unsaved man.

One day Jesus went home with him for dinner. We do not know exactly what happened, but later in the afternoon Jesus told Zacchæus he had been saved.

How did it happen? I am sure it was simply a quiet decision on the part of Zacchæus. In the presence of Christ he realized his own way of life was wrong and he definitely decided to live Christ's way. I do not think it was a great emotional upheaval. Probably there was no shouting or crying.

It is good to sing, "At the cross, where I first saw the light." But it is far better to sing, "Blessed assurance, Jesus is mine." And the important thing is not when and where you "saw the light" but rather that you now have the assurance in your heart.

Taking the Fear Out of Death

To begin with, every one of us is interested in death because we know that some day we are going to die. A lot of people are afraid of death, and their fear takes much of the joy out of living. Many refuse to think about it at all. But death is not a monster; it is our best friend, and if we could be convinced of that, life would be so much freer and happier.

Recently, I was visiting a dear old lady in the hospital. Through the years she had developed a marvelous Christian faith, and now, as the shades are swiftly being drawn for her, she said to me, "Dr. Allen, the Father's house is mighty attractive to me now." She has suffered much, and, instead of dreading death, she looks forward to it as the greatest blessing of her life. She is not the least bit afraid. On the contrary, as she is coming in sight of the other shore there is a radiant joy in her heart.

One of the greatest scientists this world has ever produced is Thomas A. Edison. He was a very exact man and was never satisfied until he had the full and final truth. His statements were always based on proved facts.

When Mr. Edison was dying, he was heard to whisper, "It is very beautiful over there."

Thomas A. Edison, a genuine scientist and scholar, would never have said that had it not been true. "It is very beautiful over there"—he was reporting what he saw.

As Robert Louis Stevenson came to his last moment on earth, he whispered, "If this is death, it is easy." Alfred Lord Tennyson was convinced that this life is the "dull side of death."

Of course, the best and surest testimony that we have is in The Book that is the truest and surest of all books. John had started with Christ as a very young man. He made a lot of mistakes, but through the years of his long life he had been faithful. Now he was exiled on the Island of Patmos—a foul place, where he was separated from those he loved and from the work so dear to his heart.

But there are always compensations for our sorrows and disappointments and, to compensate dear, old patient John, God rolled back the curtain and let him look over to the other side. What a marvelous report he gave us!

"And God shall wipe all tears from their eyes; and there shall be no more death, neither sorrow, nor crying, neither shall there be any more pain: for the former things are passed away" (Revelation 21:4).

After he had seen that, John was never afraid again. And on the basis of his sure testimony no one of us should ever fear going to a place like that.

Of course, no person in his right mind wants to die. We should want very much to live. I can speak from experience here. One night a physician told me I was going to die, and for a time I believed it. I can testify that when you come face to face with death it is not bad. I can honestly say I was not the least bit afraid.

On the other hand, I very much wanted to live. I had a wife and baby and longed to stay with them. Also, I had just started in my life's work and I wanted to continue it. That night I prayed, "Lord, I am not afraid to die yet, I very much want to live."

It is good to want to live. On the other hand, we should never let the fear of death become a dark shadow over our lives, shutting out the sunshine of God's wonderful love.

There are many reasons why we should not fear death. I will mention two.

(1) Death is the doorway to a larger life. I can understand this well because about the hardest thing in the life of any minister is moving away from a church he has served. As a pastor, you come to love the people very deeply. You baptize their babies, marry their young people, bury their loved ones. You visit the sick, comfort the sorrowing, and thrill with many who find Christ as their Saviour.

However, when it comes time to move, you think of the church to which you are going. When I came to Grace in Atlanta I hated to leave Thomson, where I had been the pastor for four years. But then I thought of being the pastor of a great church on a main thoroughfare in a big city. As I thought of the much greater opportunities, moving became a thrilling experience.

Death is like that. We hate to leave the associations and interests of this life, but then there is a larger life waiting beyond! There is something glorious and joyful about it.

(2) We need not fear death, because God is the God that He is. Think of how wise and tender God is. When He brought us into this world He planned it so beautifully. Can you think of a better way to be born than into the bosom of a mother? God made mothers. And if God so planned our birth in such a lovely fashion, we can rest assured that He has planned our entrance into the next world in some manner that will be good, even wonderful.

A mother who had lost a baby said to me, "I am so worried thinking about who will take care of it." I assured her that just as God had planned for her to take care of the precious little one in this world, we could be certain that He had just as lovingly planned for her baby's care in His great and eternal house.

This poem was found in the pocket of a Marine after a battle:

Look, God, I have never spoken to you,
But now I want to say "How do you do."
You see, God, they told me you didn't exist.
And like a fool I believed all this.

Last night from a shell hole I saw your sky.
I figured right then they had told me a lie.
Had I taken time to see things you made,
I'd have known they weren't calling a spade a spade.

I wonder, God, if you'd shake my hand.
Somehow, I feel you will understand.
Funny, I had to come to this hellish place
Before I had time to see your face.

Well, I guess there isn't much more to say,
But I'm sure glad, God, I met you today.
I guess the zero hour will soon be here,
But I'm not afraid since I know you're near.

The signal, well God, I'll have to go.
I like you lots and I want you to know.
Look, now, this will be a horrible fight
Who knows, I may come to your house tonight.

Though I wasn't friendly to you before,
I wonder, God, if you'd wait at the door.
Look, I'm crying. Me, shedding tears!
I wish I'd known you these many years.

Well, I have to go now, God, good by;
Strange, since I met you I'm not afraid to die.

(Source Unknown)

Here on this earth we are gathered together in families. Our loved ones become inexpressibly precious to us. We live in intimate associations. One gets so close to mother and father, wife or husband, sons and daughters, that they literally become a part of one's very life. Then comes a day when a strange change comes over one we love.

He is transformed before our very eyes. The light of life goes out of him. He cannot speak to us nor we to him. He is gone and we are left stunned and heartbroken. An emptiness and loneliness comes into our hearts. We broken-heartedly say, "That one whom I loved is dead." It is such a cold, hopeless thing to realize.

Then, out of the very depths of our despair, like the melody of music coming from a mighty organ, like the refreshing sound of rippling waters, comes that marvelous declaration of our Lord, "I am the resurrection, and the life: he that believeth in me, though he were dead, yet shall he live: and whosoever liveth and believeth in me shall never die" (John 11:25,26).

Then we know! We *know* we have not lost our loved ones who have died. We have been separated, and so long as we live there will be an empty place left in our hearts. To some extent, the loneliness will always be there. But when we really know that one is not forever lost, it does take away the sorrow. There is a vast difference between precious memories, loneliness, the pain of separation, on the one hand, and a sorrow that ruins and blights our lives, on the other hand.

There are several thoughts that help us when one we love has died.

(1) First, it is good to remember that death itself is not a bad experience. Some time ago there was an article in *McCall's* magazine entitled, "How Does It Feel to Die?" It was written by nine eminent physicians. The article quoted a statement by the famous Dr. William Osler, "Most human beings not only die like heroes, but, in my wide clinical experience, die really without pain or fear." All nine of the doctors agreed with that statement.

Dr. H. D. Van Fleet sums up the findings of all nine doctors. He said:

> I use the word sweetness in connection with death. As a doctor who has seen many people expire, I know it is often sweet to die. Frequently I have seen a change of expression as the moment of death approached, almost a smile, before the last breath was taken. Science cannot explain this, as science cannot explain the dynamic power which controls life. What

one may see at the point of death will probably remain an eternal mystery. But it should remain, too, a vision with no terrors for any of us.

A woman told me after a service recently that she could testify to the correctness of the above statement. She was out swimming in the ocean and was pulled under. She was in the very process of drowning, and almost did drown. But just before she lost consciousness, the one thought that filled her mind was this: "Mama will worry about me, but I wish she knew how easy it is."

When we realize that death was really an easy and happy experience for our loved one, that helps a lot.

(2) A second thought that helps is that perhaps death was a blessing for our loved one. A dear friend told me this experience. Her husband was very ill and the doctor told her he was dying. The children became almost hysterical and began to scream, "Mama, pray; mama, pray; mama, pray." She knelt and prayed fervently, "Lord, spare my husband's life. Don't let him die." Even as she spoke a change came over him, his pulse grew stronger, he opened his eyes.

He lived for nine years after that. But he lived in horribly excruciating pain. Nearly every breath he took was torture. His wife told me, "There have been no less than a thousand times when I regretted asking God not to let him die. I realize so well how foolish my request was."

There are many things worse than death, and I rather think that, instead of becoming harsh and bitter when we have lost a loved one, we might better have faith in the goodness and mercy of God. Only God can know all the facts. Instead of hating God for letting some loved one die, we might later thank Him with all our heart.

(3) Jesus said, "Whosoever liveth and believeth in me shall never die." Death is not the end, it is really the beginning of life. The Bible is a wonderful book. It is so gentle and kind. Through His Word, God tries to tell us something of the glories of the new life on the other side. But it is beyond our understanding. We just cannot imagine how wonderful that life really is. So we are told, "Eye hath not seen, nor ear heard, neither have entered into the heart of man, the things which God hath prepared for them that love him" (I Corinthians 2:9).

People do not come back from the other side. Perhaps they cannot come back. On the other hand, perhaps they do not want to come back. Whatever life on the other side may be like, we can be sure our loved ones are enjoying a happier and larger life than they had on this side.

My own father died just after midnight in an Atlanta hospital. I loved him very deeply. He was a minister, and we were very close. I lived at Douglasville, about twenty-five miles from Atlanta, and early that morning I was driving home. A nauseating despondency had settled over me. But as I went over a hill I saw the sunrise in all its glory. Then I thought of that lovely song, "Sunrise tomorrow, sunrise tomorrow . . . sunrise with Jesus for eternity."

Then, like the dawn, a truth of tremendous import burst upon me. "Why, the sunrise has come for one whom

I love." That very moment his passing became all right for me.

Arthur Brisbane pictured a crowd of grieving caterpillars carrying a dead cocoon to its final resting place. The poor, distressed caterpillars were weeping and heartbroken. But all the while the lovely butterfly fluttered happily over their heads!

The most hopeful and helpful words about life after death for me are the words Christ spoke to the penitent man who was dying that day by His side. "Today shalt thou be with me in paradise" (Luke 23:43). Here are three great affirmations:

(1) *Today* . . . After Lazarus had died, Jesus said to Martha, "Thy brother shall rise again." But Martha replied, "I know that he shall rise again in the resurrection at the last day." She gets little comfort from the thought of a resurrection in some dim, distant future. Then Jesus replied, "I am the resurrection, and the life: he that believeth in me, though he were dead, yet shall he live; and whosoever liveth and believeth in me shall never die" (John 11:23-26).

Jesus is saying that the resurrection comes immediately after death. Today—today—today.

We go to the cemetery where the bodies of our loved are buried. It is a sweet and a sacred spot for us, yet our loved ones are not there. They never have been there. When we pay reverence at a grave, when we put undue significance on a cemetery, we are utterly missing the Christian message. Our loved ones are in eternity, not in some cold grave.

(2) *Thou shalt be with me* . . . Thou—me. We will

be the same people over there as we are here. When Jesus called Lazarus from the grave, He said, "Lazarus, come forth" (John 11:43). He did not say, "James, come forth," or "John, come forth." He was Lazarus on this side, he was Lazarus on the other side. Jesus said to Martha, "Thy brother shall rise again" (John 11:23). Even though he had passed on, he was *still* her brother.

After death, Jesus Himself had the same loving features and was recognized by those who had known Him. He had the same nail prints in His hands. He had the same loves. He was the same beyond the grave as He was before the grave.

I know the fact of recognition after death presents difficulties, but without that assurance eternal life would mean very little. Before I was born, my mother and father had a little girl, Ruth, who died. Though the years came and went, they never completely gave up Ruth. Her little picture was on the mantle through the years. I think I know how they felt.

Some years ago my wife and I were separated from our oldest son for some weeks. We missed him very much and I will never forget the night we finally returned home. Somebody could have changed the doors and put in their stead doors made of pearl. The floors might have been overlaid with gold while we were gone. But we would not have noticed that. As we went into the house we wanted to see our baby, and, if he had not been there, no matter how fine the house might have been, it would not have been home for us.

And as my father entered the eternal city of God, I know it made no difference to him whether or not the gates were of pearl. He did not care whether the streets were of gold or concrete. What he wanted was to see his baby. And if his baby had not been there and if he had not known her, no matter what else might have been there, it would not have been heaven for him.

We will see our loved ones again.

(3) *In paradise.* I think Jesus meant the same thing that we mean by heaven. I do not think there is an intermediary place. And what a glorious thing it is to think of what heaven is like. It is so grand and glorious that our small, finite minds cannot fully comprehend it. And, in fact, it means different things to different people.

There was Fanny Crosby. She was blind all her life and when she dreamed of heaven I think she wrote her finest song: "Some day the silver chord will break, and I no more as now shall sing; but O the joy when I shall wake, within the palace of my King. And I shall *see* Him face to face." It was for her a place where she could see.

As St. John looked into heaven, the first thing he saw was that "there was no more sea" (Revelation 21:1). He was exiled on Patmos. The sea was his prison. The sea kept him from doing what he wanted to do and being what he wanted to be. The sea was his handicap. In heaven there are no more handicaps.

After a service recently, a man who had lost both his hands in an accident asked me, "When I get to heaven will I have some hands?" That is what heaven means to him.

Last year I buried a beautiful young lady. That is, she was beautiful physically, but terribly handicapped mentally. Her mind never did develop, and after the service her mother who loved her more than life itself said, "I am so happy because now I know her handicap has been removed."

All of us have handicaps of some kind. There are things we want to do, but have not the ability or opportunity here to do them. But over there the handicaps will be taken away, and we will be able both to be and to do all on which our heart is set.

"Today shalt thou be with me in paradise." What a glorious and happy thought that is!

One of Carl Sandburg's greatest books is his *Prairie Years,* the early life of Abraham Lincoln. In it he describes life on the great prairies of the Middle West during the pioneer days. Life was extremely hard for the pioneers, and their hands became gnarled, says Sandburg, "like the roots of the old oak tree."

Medical resources were meager, and sickness and death were their ever-present enemies. One fourth of all their babies died. Malaria and milk sickness were plagues that killed thousands. Nancy Hanks, Lincoln's own mother, died of milk sickness, as did one of his sisters and her baby.

Sandburg tells about those difficult days, but also he tells that on the Lord's day they would go to the crude churches they had built to hear some pioneer, circuit-riding preacher and sing together:

> There's a land that is fairer than day,
> And by faith we can see it afar;
> For the Father waits over the way,
> To prepare us a dwelling place there.

And he declares that was the faith that kept them going, that built America and made America great.

The last time I was in Mobile I went around to see a friend whom I appreciate and admire very much, George Downing. After George finished Emory, he went with the Coca-Cola Company and made an outstanding record. At the close of the war he was sent to Europe in a responsible position. He went ahead and got a place to live, then his lovely young wife and their two precious little girls took seats on a plane to join him. But on the way over the airplane crashed into a mountain, and, along with a number of others, they perished.

We held a simple memorial service for them, and in the days following George and I were together a lot. I wanted to do something for him, but he did far more for me. Not one word of bitterness did he ever speak. In no way did he become harsh or ugly. His heart was broken, but his spirit was magnificent.

We lived at Thomson, Georgia, and at the time we were building a new Sunday-school building. One day George said, "I would like to furnish the nursery, kindergarten, and primary rooms in memory of those I love." He went on to tell how much Sunday school had meant to his little girls, and now that they were in the Father's house above he wanted to do something in the Father's house here on earth which would be an inspiration to other little girls and boys.

He bought a lot of things—small chairs and tables, a tiny organ and a little piano, toys of all kinds, a record player and a library of records, books children would like, and lovely pictures for the walls.

Now George is married again, and they have a little baby. He is working, he is happy, he is living a great life. And that is just as it should be. Sorrows and disappointments come, more to some than to others, but to some extent to every one. But out of the sorrows come lovely and beautiful things. Those we have lost inspire us to grander and nobler living, and, instead of becoming bitter, we become better. And life goes on.

I used to play baseball, and my father went to the games because he was always interested in whatever his children did. I remember one game especially. It was a tight game, and I happened to get a long hit. I was running around the bases as fast as I could, but I seemed to gain added strength when I heard him shouting above the crowd, "Come on home, Charles, come on home." Since he has been gone, there have been times when the going was a little harder for me and I have been tempted to do less than my best, but then I could hear him saying, "Come on home, Charles, come on home."

The pull of a loved one who is now in the home above often is our very strongest influence.

Florence Jones Hadley has said it beautifully in her poem:

I think ofttimes as the night draws nigh
Of an old house on the hill,
Of a yard all wide and blossom-starred
Where the children played at will.
And when at last the night came down,
Hushing their merry din,
Mother would look around and ask,
"Are all the children in?"

'Tis many and many a year since then,
And the old house on the hill
No longer echoes to childish feet
And the yard is now so still.
But I see it all, as the shadows creep,
And though many the years have been,
I still can hear my mother ask,
"Are all the children in?"

I wonder if when the shadows fall
On the last, short earthly day,
When we say good by to the world outside,
All tired with our childish play;
When we step out into that other land
Where mother so long has been,
Will we hear her ask, just as of old,
"Are all the children in?"

Many people are walking around on this earth who are dead or partly dead. Their hopes are dead. Their dreams and ideals are dead. Someone once wrote a poem about a wild duck. He could fly high and far, but one day he landed in a barnyard. There life was less exciting but easier. The duck began to eat and live with the tame ducks and gradually he forgot how to fly. He became fat and lazy.

In the spring and fall, however, as the wild ducks flew overhead, something stirred inside him, but he could not rise to join them. The poem ends with these lines:

He's a pretty good duck for the shape he's in,
But he isn't the duck that he might have been.

The great prophet Ezekiel told us long ago that "the soul that sinneth, it shall die" (18:4). St. Paul warned us that "the wages of sin is death" (Romans 6:23). The most tragic death is not physical death. It is the death of the soul, the death of the personality, the dying of something fine inside of one.

We need only to remember the story of Belshazzar the night of his great feast. In his drunken stupor Belshazzar "commanded to bring the golden and silver vessels which his father Nebuchadnezzar had taken out of the temple which was in Jerusalem; that the king and the princes might drink therein."

Even in his wildest moments, Nebuchadnezzar had not dared to lay his profane hands on the sacred vessels from the temple of the eternal God, but his godless son did it and that night a hand appeared and wrote on the wall, "Mene, mene, tekel, upharsin." The king's face went white. He was scared into soberness, and he immediately sent for the preacher. He had not wanted the preacher around before, but now he needed him. Daniel translated the words on the wall for him: "Thou art weighed in the balances, and art found wanting" (Daniel 5:27).

Many people have desecrated the high and holy things in their lives, and, little by little, have died until—on God's side of the scales—there is little left.

But listen to these glorious words of our Lord: "I am the resurrection and the life. He that believeth in me, though he were dead, yet shall he live."

In Korea they call a Christian a "resurrected" person. They mean that the Christian's soul had almost died, but, somehow, he had allowed the spirit of Christ to come in, believed in Him, responded to that belief, and began to live again.

Once they were building a new highway in England. It was to run between Holborn and the Strand. In the way stood a very, very old building. The workmen tore it down and cleared off the ground on which it stood. After the ground had been exposed to the sunshine and rain for some months, a wonderful thing happened. Flowers began to spring up, and botanists and naturalists from all over England came to study them. Many of the flowers were identified as plants the Romans had brought to England almost 2,000 years before. Some of the plants that sprang up are completely unknown today.

Hidden there in the ground, without air and light, the seeds seemed to have died. But they were not dead. As soon as the obstacles were cleared away, and the sunshine let in, they sprang into the fulness of their beauty.

So the seeds of eternal life are in every human life. But often those seeds are buried under such things as unbelief, selfishness, pride, lust, preoccupation, or some other sin. But when in humility and with child-like faith we bow before Him, it is the resurrection and the life for us. Marvelous things happen within our souls and we become finer and better than ever we had dared to hope. Life takes on for us a new meaning, a new radiance and beauty, a new happiness, and peace becomes ours. We live again.

Some time ago, when it was announced that I was to preach in a series of revival services in a certain town in another state, I received a letter from a couple living there inviting, even insisting, that I stay in their home. I was surprised, because when I was their pastor in other years they had had little use or time for me. Life had become too tame for them at that time, and they began doing a lot of things that were wrong. Little by little they had let their highest ideals and dreams die. They had stopped coming to church.

When I arrived they greeted me with the very warmest cordiality. They gave me the nicest room in the house, there were lovely flowers on the dresser and a luscious basket of fruit on the table. Everything they could possibly do for my comfort they did. She even insisted on serving my breakfast in my room for my convenience.

They had not been attending church, but they both went that night. At the close of the service, as I always do in revivals, I gave a call for prayer at the altar. This couple came. They lingered longer than any others. I watched them, and I could tell it was not easy, but there that night at the altar they prayed through. I was with them the rest of that week, and have seen them many times since. Being well acquainted with them, I know that once they had died, and then had risen again. A new life is now theirs, a new joy and a new peace.

It was not me they wanted to honor in their home that week. They had simply come to see that the things they had sneered at and turned their backs on in years gone by were the things that really mattered most. They wanted to get back what they had lost, and they did.

I see that same thing happen every Sunday night as hundreds of people pray at the altar of Grace Church. Hundreds have told me after our night service that they had been lost and now were found, once were dead but now are alive.

Life—eternal life—is here, right now, for all who will accept it.

Above all things, do not miss our Lord's first Easter message. According to St. Mark 16:7, it was, "Go, tell his disciples and Peter."

Tell His disciples! Those who ran away when He was arrested. Who made no protest at His trial. The disciples who quit and went back to fishing. Who were not loyal when they were needed so badly.

Yes, and tell all His disciples today who once started with Him but found the going hard and gave up and quit. Tell those who have turned their backs on the better way, who have lowered their standards and have shamefully failed. Tell those who have lost their inspiration to live their best, those who have lost hope and whose lives have been shattered. Tell every person who would like to try again that Jesus is risen and there is a new chance.

Among the disciples was "doubting" Thomas. He had become confused in his thinking, had lost his faith, and could not accept the testimony of others.

Yes, and tell all those who have difficulty in believing. Whose faith is a bit shaky and whose doubts are very real. Tell them that Jesus is not angry because of their doubts. Instead, He comes tenderly and sympathetically to restore faith and bring certainty. He wants it told to all who doubt that He is risen.

". . . and Peter," He said. I am so glad He named Peter. The disciple who promised that though all others would forsake Christ, he would remain loyal. Yet at the very moment Christ was on trial Peter stood by the fire "warming himself." His own comforts he put above his loyalty to Christ. He broke his promise. Yet Jesus especially wanted Peter to know He had risen. That He was ever ready to forget the past and give Peter a new chance.

Yes, tell every person who started but for some reason quit. Tell those who made promises but broke them. Tell every person who has failed, who has sinned, who would receive forgiveness, that the Christ of the second chance is here and ready to start with him again.

Yes, and tell all those who have difficulty in accepting a future life. Tell them that Christ is risen and that He said, "Because I live, ye shall live also" (John 14:19). Also that He said, "Whosoever liveth and believeth in me shall never die" (John 11:26).

The Easter message robs death of its terror and promises a solution to life's mysteries. The great Beethoven became deaf and could not hear his own music. However, he declared, "It is the hope of immortality with its brighter future that inspires me to keep on trying."

And Beethoven's biographer wrote, "With the shadows of the dark valley closing around him, he could look to the Land of Promise beyond, and with a mighty triumph sing of the joy and victory which surely awaited him in a world where the wrongs of earth are righted at last."

Why did that baby die, or that young husband get killed, or any of the great disappointments of life have to be? I do not know the answer, but because of Easter I do know there is an answer and that some day it will all be made plain.

Finally, the assurance of eternity is our greatest incentive to a life of consecrated service.

James Chalmers, after twenty-one hard years as a missionary, said, "Recall the twenty-one years, give me back its shipwrecks, its standings in the face of death, the savages knocking me to the ground and beating me with clubs, give it back to me and I will still be your missionary."

DATE DUE